Circles

Nurture and grow your creative gift

Elisabeth Pike

O&U

Onwards & Upwards

Onwards and Upwards Publishers

3 Radfords Turf, Cranbrook, Exeter,
EX5 7DX, United Kingdom.
www.onwardsandupwards.org

First edition, published in the United Kingdom by Onwards and Upwards Publishers (2019).

ISBN: 978-1-78815-733-9
Typeface: Sabon LT
Graphic design: LM Graphic Design

Printed in the United Kingdom.

Endorsements

In this book Liz uses her own life story and situation to bring the true heart of a creative person into focus. The highs and lows, the struggles and breakthroughs, are woven into this book to help support, inspire and give life to the creative nature in the reader. Liz describes true life situations that she has had to navigate to pursue a 'God-given' calling and gift. She has remembered and recorded some precious moments of her life journey to share.

This book can stimulate latent creative yearnings and awaken some to the creative potential they have or carry, especially in a faith-based setting where creative expression is not always seen as a 'valid' part of faith. In places you can sense the creative heart of God literally speaking/calling/shouting to the reader to explore, create, continue and wrestle with carrying creative burdens and ideas they have.

Colin Brice
Founder and Leader of Eden People
www.edenpeople.org.uk

I first read a draft of Liz's book when I was in the murky depths of early years motherhood. To say the book was timely is an understatement. Despite the obvious joys of parenthood, I had lost myself in raising three children under the age of four. As a musician and writer, I struggled not to resent motherhood for depriving me of the creative flow that is fundamental to my being. Liz's book brought such perspective, hope and challenge. She had written what was in my heart with an eloquence that I do not possess. Liz's book is a call to all those creatives feeling lost under the pressures of motherhood. Her writing will revitalise your creative practice with the combined sharpness of an academic mind; and the warmth of a good friend who has just made you a well-needed cup of tea. You won't regret reading it.

Rebecca Hitch
Musician and Writer

Elisabeth has faithfully persevered through challenges, struggles and trials to develop and express her creative gift. Recounting her experiences with honesty and vulnerability, she calls and encourages us all to discover our own unique, God-given creativity and significance. Whilst written with particular encouragement in the area of creativity, this book contains lessons and encouragements for us all to step out and grow in all that God calls us to be.

Joy Ahearn
Leader of Guildford Community Church

Liz Pike's encouragement for us to pursue our creative dreams and find ways of expressing them is a creative work of art in itself. It follows her life in Guildford and Shrewsbury as a struggling young Mum (now with four children), her second child being diagnosed with Type 1 diabetes, and her husband, also a creative musician, also struggling to make ends meet. Yet through it all there is the same quiet, compelling call to creativity, which Liz shares with us. Her children and life are part of this, in a background which often seems to work against any time at all for creative expression. Each chapter nevertheless includes one or more of her poems which arise out of the often perplexing cross-currents of her life.

The book is a treasure trove of many wonderful quotations from a wide range of writers on the mystery of creativity. At the same time, the book is full of practical suggestions, the more convincing because arising from her own life as described in the book. And through everything there is the encouragement that listening and giving expression to the creative gift within us is what God calls us to, as underlined by frequent references to the scriptures, brought to life by the new context in which they are placed. This thread running throughout the book rises to a glorious climax in the closing lines of the final chapter: triumphant without being triumphalistic.

Liz has provided a great service to everyone who has ever wondered if they have a creative gift inside them but has lacked the courage to pursue it. A copy of this book should be close to hand to each of us.

Peter Wilkinson
Pastor, Teacher and Writer

Circles is a book that will grab you and draw you in to a world of creativity. Liz uses her life experiences to draw the parallels between creativity and parenthood, in that in both we beget a being that is of us, but which has a life of its own. Expressing the profound life-giving nature of the creative process in a book (which itself is so creative) is a gift to anyone who feels the stirring of the creative urge. Buy this book and be inspired.

Rev. Richard Spencer
Team Vicar
All Saints' Church, Ashdon

Liz Pike writes with passion, spiritual integrity and searing honesty. She not only describes her own personal journey in embracing creativity but draws on the wisdom of well-loved poets and writers to explore the ambiguities and joys of the art of writing. Her poetry, which resonates with Celtic spirituality, expresses wonderfully the moments of inspiration and struggle of everyday life, in beautiful imagery and imaginative use of language.

It has been a privilege to accompany Liz on her creative journey over the past ten years and to witness how, against so many odds, including the increasing challenges and demands of motherhood, she has made space for the seeds of creativity within her to grow, blossom and bear fruit – not just in this book and other published writing, but in the lives of many others. A commissioned writer myself, I read *Circles* at a time when my confidence had waned and I lacked the courage to take on a bigger writing challenge. Liz's words were exactly what I needed for God to speak again to me: that if I didn't write what I had inside me, who else would? I encourage you to read Circles with an open heart and mind, and to receive the creative call yourself. May you be inspired and encouraged by the authenticity of Liz's words, life and testimony – and may the wonderful Creator's glory shine through you.

Carol Herzig
Teacher; former Editor of *Inspiring Women Every Day*
and Freelance Writer

About the Author

 Liz Pike lives in Shropshire with her husband and four children. She writes short stories, fiction and poetry and teaches creative writing to adults and children. Her work has been published in *The Guardian, Third Way, Fractured West,* and in *JUNO magazine* amongst others. She sells her hand-lettered poetry prints in her Etsy shop where she also takes commissions. *There You Are,* her book of 34 original hand-lettered poems about motherhood, is available from her Etsy shop and Amazon. She also writes on creativity and faith. She has previously worked as a bookseller and librarian and has completed a Master's in Creative Writing from Goldsmiths University, London. She likes cities, long train journeys, and old photographs.

TUMBLR

elisabethpike.tumblr.com

ETSY

etsy.com/uk/shop/LittleBirdEditions

FACEBOOK

facebook.com/littlebirdeditions
facebook.com/ElisabethPikeWriter
facebook.com/writefromtheheartshropshire

INSTAGRAM

instagram.com/elisabethpikewrites
instagram.com/writefromtheheartshropshire
instagram.com/littlebirdeditions

TWITTER

twitter.com/elisabethpike

This book is for my parents,
for giving me space to grow and dream
when I was a child;

for my four children,
Sam, Ivy, Ben and Annie,
for teaching me how to love;

and for Joel,
my companion on this journey,
who always cheers me on,
always believes in me and
who walks out this creative call with me,
day by day by day.
I love you.

Circles

Contents

Circles

Preface

WHO ARE THOSE CRAZY DREAMERS WHO PLUG AWAY AT something, hour after hour on their own, believing that one day it will come to light? I am one of them, holding on for years to a quiet faith that my writing would eventually see the light of day. And now, as you are reading this, my prayers and faith have come to something and seeds are slowly spreading.

It sometimes seems to me that creatives are a species apart. When we despair, people may say with frustration, 'Just get a regular job!' but inside of each of us creative labourers there is this voice and a quiet determination that says, *I will do it, I can do it,* and there is a reason why. It isn't for vanity's sake; rather it is to make sense of the world, to listen to what our hearts are telling us, to put words on our wonder.

I think of writers (insert here artists, musicians, dancers...) like athletes sometimes, training for a marathon, putting in the hours day in, day out, maybe getting their five minutes of glory if they do well on the day when it matters, maybe crashing out due to injury, but still going back to training, putting in the hours, and still believing that their day will come, still believing that this is what they were born for. Anne Lamott, in *Bird by Bird,* said:

> *I heard a preacher say recently that hope is a revolutionary patience; let me add that so is being a writer. Hope begins in the dark, the stubborn hope that if you just show up and try to do the right thing, the dawn will come. You wait and you watch and you work, you don't give up.*[1]

I completely agree with her here. Stubborn hope sounds good to me.

We didn't ask for this burden of creativity, but it has been given to us. Should we choose to accept its mantel in our lives, it becomes like an instinct or urge to create that can't be suppressed, and no matter how many times we try to be 'normal' and turn our back on it, it won't leave us alone, like the way my cat follows me around the house when she wants to be fed, and just sits just behind me silently. She waits there as if

---

[1] Lamott, Anne; *Bird by Bird;* Anchor Books, 1994 (p.xxiii).

to say, 'When are you going to pay attention to me?' But what if, in these moments of creation, we become dangerously like our Father and a lightning rod of synergy between heaven and earth? What if earth is longing for moments like this?

This book was born from a desire to articulate my own creative journey and the struggles and joys I have met along the way. The journey is by no means over and I have by no means arrived, but as a fellow creative, I say to you today: what you have inside you to create is of immense value and if you don't find a way to say it, perhaps no one will.

Enter into this exploration of the creative call with me and watch it unfurl and grow in you. Say yes to the creative call in your life, join with the circles of those who have been before and of those who are yet to come. We are in this together.

1

The Call

How blessed is the man whose strength is in You,
In whose heart are the highways to Zion.[2]

ARE YOU READY TO JUMP TWO FEET AT ONCE, TO PURSUE
the desires of your heart, believing that God is the one who placed them
there in the first place? Think of this book as a creative handbook, a
manual for getting back to the heart of it, the quietened dreams in your
heart, the secret longings that have been hushed. It is time to take your
heart seriously, to listen to yourself and what you have got to say, to give
yourself time to hone your gifts, to open your mouth, your heart, to dare
to share the creations that are stirring inside you. Your significance on
earth is far bigger than you could ever imagine; there is only one
expression of God on this earth that looks like you.

We were born to reflect God's glory here on earth. It is a deep
conviction of mine that when we soak in God's truth and turn it into art,
whether it be a song, a painting, or a piece of writing, the resulting works
carry a deep and powerful message because they combine the truth of our
testimony and a touch of the glory of God. There is a rhythm, like a wave
which flows from him, and this song is sung through all creation. But it's
when we choose to let the same rhythm come out of us and through us
that we connect with the eternal song and let creation know who we are.

These days, there are so many associations that people make with
'Christian' or 'church' or 'God'. It's as if automatic barriers fling up, of
past hurts, misconceptions, bad experiences, so that everything we say
afterwards is interpreted through a veil of individual experience. Church
is a group of human beings, so it is bound to get things wrong. People
will misunderstand and offend each other; they will disagree over certain

---

[2] Psalm 84:5 (NASB).

things. *But God.* That is why we are here. To know him, to hear him speak into our lives, to show him to others. And when we share a dance, a film, a poem, or a drawing that comes from the heart of the artist, and from the heart of God, we can see it for what it is. The truth behind it speaks louder and speaks to the heart without the objections of the head.

When I think of the creative life, I think of the natural life, the circles that we live through: autumn, winter, spring, summer; longing, conception, pregnancy, labour and birth. Growing, walking and resting. It's this whole thing about being on a journey. We are all going somewhere. God has called us to walk through this life, not to remain as we are but to shift and to grow. I love the verse quoted above from Psalm 84. There is a commitment in our lives to keep growing. It is a discipline to learn and to grow as a Christian. If God speaks to us through something, we can choose to treasure it close to our hearts and then it will transform our lives, like a seed planted in fertile soil. I equally love another translation of this verse:

> *Blessed are those whose strength is in you, whose hearts are set on pilgrimage.*[3]

This pilgrimage speaks of our lives, a journey walked with him.

So may we walk with our God, may we live in the rhythms of his grace, may we be bold in our creativity, may we dare, may we live beautifully and boldly, knowing who we are. A wonderful passage in Ben Okri's *Astonishing the Gods* seems to sum up the creative walk for me. As Christians and artists, we are reaching into the heavenlies; we are bringing seeds of heaven down to earth and this is amazing.

> *On the whole, big things are small for us [...]. The most difficult thing for us is to do things which achieve permanence in the higher universe and which are unseen and can never therefore be destroyed. Our highest acts of creativity are in the empty spaces, in the air, in dreams, in unseen realms. There we have our cities, our castles, our greatest books, our great music, our art, our science, our truest love, our fullest sustenance [...]. And sometimes [...] our highest creative acts, our highest playfulness, our self-overcoming, our purest art, our ascending songs, by some mysterious grace transcend so*

---

[3] NIV.

many boundaries and enter so many realms that we occasionally astonish even the gods [...]. And even our way and our discoveries are still young in all their possibilities. We wake every day in a state of absolute humility and joyfulness at all that lies possible before us [...]. Therefore we have no fame. We live quietly [...]. We do not want to be remembered, or praised. We only want to increase the light, and to spread illumination.[4]

This speaks to me as a creative; this desire to achieve permanence, to create something ethereal, something above this oft mundane life. What a call to arms (to pens, to brushes) for the creative; to go forth and dream with our eyes open, to bring the sounds of heaven down to earth! We wake with joy at all that lies before us... What a challenge and an honour.

---

[4] Okri, Ben; *Astonishing the Gods;* Phoenix House, 1995 (p.148).

2

Space to Dream

IT IS RARE TO HAVE THE HUSH OF AN EMPTY HOUSE ALL TO myself. But right now, all I can hear is the hum of the computer screen, the creak of a door being slammed outside, the footsteps of the cat coming in and going out. My heart rate slows.

All morning my husband and I have been cooped up with the children, in our tiny house in the June rain. We have been winding ourselves up and up. I don't understand why sometimes it is harder when we are both here, why we are not allowed to have a conversation together, why my son makes that awful screeching noise as soon as we try to talk. And so, at the peak of another dispute, I slam down the lid of the biscuit tin, and march off with my half-eaten cookie. I almost cry, but I am too tired. And so instead, I get into bed and wait until my husband comes up and says that he will take the kids out and I hear the back door slam and the silence in the house descend. I feel guilty and immensely thankful at once. Some days I wonder if I will go insane.

I have been realising what I'm missing lately. As a writer and a mother, I crave time, but not just any old time. If I'm out with just my youngest in the pushchair, I have time, of a sort. I have space to think, I have a break from her chirps, because when she is in the pushchair, she just looks or sleeps. I have the buzz of normal life around me. I might wander aimlessly around shops, and if I'm at home and she's sleeping, I will clean, which, for some reason, seems nobler to me than to do what I really want to do which is to write. And if I don't feel too exhausted in the evenings, I will attempt to get on with writing.

But last night, after tidying, I sat down to watch the news and then my daughter woke with a temperature. And an hour later, there I was typing in my bedroom, my son asleep behind me on the bed, my daughter crying for me in the other room. Even when they are asleep (or supposed to be asleep) they tend to encroach upon every corner of my life.

And even when all goes to plan; when they are both asleep in their beds, I boot up the computer, sure that by the time my fingers hit the keys, I will have achieved some inspiration or have some inkling of where to take my story next. But in reality, I often sit there with a blank screen and a blank mind, thinking of the things I need to pick up the next day at Sainsbury's.

What I want is the daytime; to be sitting at a desk in a room with a cup of tea and the sunlight streaming in. I want to be able to have my notepads lined up at the back of the desk. I want to have all the books that I so love lined up in front of me, my heroes to cheer me on to the finish line. I want to have the willpower to not 'google' things at the drop of a hat but to make a list and do it later. I want time that is set aside, precious and protected even though I might not achieve anything.

I long for time when I am awake enough that, should a moment of clarity come surging through, then I would be ready and waiting for it. One day, I will have this time, but perhaps not yet. Time is certainly the greatest luxury that I took for granted before I became a parent.

There is another baby on the way, after our lovely two, a boy and a girl. I adore his independence, growing like that all by himself, without me even suspecting for two months. The audacity, the beauty! So it will be a long time, I fear, before I am able to sit like I dream of doing, at a table, with a window, in the daytime. And to think that I did it all those years ago and didn't realise my good fortune. I handed in my notice to the bookshop where I was working because I was angry at the management and thought I was making a statement. Shot myself in the foot, rather; gave myself 'the fear' a little too much. And then I had it; a desk and an empty house all day long. I was doing an MA in Creative Writing and told myself that it would look okay on my CV, but in reality, we couldn't afford the rent. Knowing that it would only be for a short time, I did try to make the most of it, but I didn't perceive it as the shining jewel that it was. I was scared by it; I was depressed by it. I held it at arm's length, when I should have just got on with it and written for all that I was worth. Looking back, I don't think I was ready for the solitude.

But then maybe I had not quite become myself fully, for I feel that I became more of myself when I became a mother. More, and at the same time less. I seemed to lose my sense of identity; there was no choice but to give up everything to go to the children in the night-time, and sometimes even my husband seemed to come second to them. But at the same time, I became stronger; I realised that I could cope and keep going/inventing/sticking/feeding; that there is no such thing as a mummy sick day.

There have been times whilst sitting on the carpet playing Duplo when a poem has flitted through the room like a butterfly. I have heard a brief line of it before it has flown out of the window and gone; forgotten or trampled over, before I had the time to snatch it and write it down. And for a while I thought, *fine, let them go, there is no time to catch them.* But now I am ready to wait for them again.

And of course, we can always long to be at a different stage than the one we are in, and we all need patience to survive the toughest and most intense times. I don't think it makes any sense to wish away our lives, we must accept the season that we are in. The early years of parenting are intense but also short-lived, and there will be time again, one day. What I am advocating, rather, is keeping a little space for yourself, a little headspace, dreaming space. Keep yourself alive, keep your dreams alive. There may not be time today, but there will be time soon.

A thing that often goes unacknowledged is that adversity is often strangely motivating when it comes to creativity. When you crave time, you really make the most of the time that you are given. When we were living in Guildford, before having children, I worked in a job that was okay and just about paid the bills, but I wasn't thriving; I always said that what I really wanted to be doing was writing, but I wasn't writing with any gusto because there weren't any deadlines, there was no urgency. This has changed as I have got older, and as my time has become a more precious commodity. I long for time to write now, and when I get it, I write for all I am worth.

But there is grace too. I have heard it said that writing is as much about staring at the empty page as it is about hitting keys, and I love that. It takes the pressure off; it gives permission to dream. It allows for the fact that the words have a life of their own, as Nabokov said in *Lectures on Literature,* that they will arrive when they are ready:

> *...the pages are still blank, but there is a miraculous feeling of the words being there, written in invisible ink and clamouring to become visible.*[5]

I have seen this with several of my stories, that you write through the unknowing and things just write themselves into happening before you,

---

[5] Nabokov, Vladimir; *Lectures on Literature;* Harvest Books, 1982 (p.379).

underneath your pen. It is the most wonderful thing. I love the thought of the story having its own existence, and that our job as writers is to listen and wait for it; a bit like the new baby arriving, settling in my womb, announcing quietly that he was there through my sudden distaste for tea.

Virginia Woolf notes this necessity of waiting, of making space to dream, in *A Room of One's Own:*

> *By hook or by crook, I hope that you will do whatever it takes to possess yourselves of money enough to travel and to idle, to contemplate the future or the past of the world, to dream over books and loiter at street corners and let the line of thought dip deep into the stream.*[6]

Did you hear that? To idle! Yes, I say. Yes to that. My husband, the composer *Tiny Leaves,* found the lack of time and space a catalyst for creativity as illustrated in his EP *In These Narrow Spaces* which spoke of this tension. And of course there is always beauty to be found, whether we are losing the plot whilst staying at home looking after toddlers, or bored to tears in a day job that just pays the rent. A poet who shows this wonderfully is Fred Voss, who finds inspiration on the shop floor of a metal workshop. In *Poetry Jackpot,* he paints such a vivid picture of seeing and not seeing, the distinction is quite beautiful:

> *I wish the machinists around me in this shop could feel the joy*
> *I feel each morning as I wait for the poems to come to me. [...]*
> *I cannot wait to open my toolbox each morning and look for*
> *poems [...] while these machinists around me drag their feet*
> *like they are dead.*[7]

For the beauty is always there, he says, you just have to take the time, open your eyes and perceive it. But then, Virginia Woolf says in *A Room of One's Own* that this is the great gift of an artist: the seeing where others do not see:

> *What is meant by 'reality'? It would seem to be something very erratic, very undependable – now to be found in a dusty road, now in a scrap of newspaper in the street, now a daffodil in the sun. [...] It overwhelms one walking home beneath the*

---

[6] Woolf, Virginia; *A Room of One's Own;* Penguin, 2000 [1920] (p.98).

[7] Voss, Fred; *Poetry Jackpot;* published in Ambit No. 203, Winter 2011.

stars and makes the silent world more real than the world of speech [...]. Now the writer, as I think, has the chance to live more than other people in the presence of this reality. It is his business to find it and collect it and communicate it to the rest of us.[8]

Similarly, Raymond Carver notes, in his essay 'On Writing', this importance of seeing what others do not see, of taking the time, of putting it down on the page:

...a writer sometimes needs to be able to stand and gape at this or that thing – a sunset or an old shoe – in absolute and simple amazement.[9]

How wonderful our mission statement as creatives! To live, to see, to idle, to communicate wonder! For there is the space to create but also the permission to dream. The Indian chief Smohalla said:

My young men shall never work. Men who work cannot dream; and wisdom comes to us in dreams.[10]

What a beautiful idea, to value the dream over the toil of life. And if there is a dream in your heart, then you must fight for it. Listen to what the apostle Paul said in the letter to the Hebrews:

Therefore, since we are surrounded by such a great cloud of witnesses, let us throw off everything that so easily entangles, and let us run the race marked out for us.[11]

Whatever the race marked out for you is, run it, go headlong into it. I know that for me, my race is to write.

Dreaming lengthens the perspective; it opens up all sorts of possibilities. I write out scenarios in my journal, imagining five years from now, what I hope to have achieved, the house I dream of owning then. The space and permission to dream is my little bit of reclaiming myself, of putting back up the boundaries to my life that have been taken down and trampled on by toddlers. I need time, a silent pause in the

[8] Woolf, Virginia; *A Room of One's Own;* Penguin, 2000 [1920] (p.99).
[9] Carver, Raymond; 'On Writing', *Fires;* Vintage, 2009 [1977] (p.23).
[10] McLuhan, T.C.; *Touch the Earth: A Self-Portrait of Indian Existence;* Promontory Press, 1991 (p.56).
[11] Hebrews 12:1 (NIV).

barrage of words spoken at me simultaneously, to think coherent thoughts that do not get snatched away mid-flight. And if all this takes is two hours at a desk in the morning, then that is what I am fighting for.

The early Christian poet Caedmon couldn't sing in tune but loved to hear others worshipping. He was visited by an angel who gave him a beautiful voice to sing which radically changed the direction of his life. A liturgy remembering him called 'In Declaration of a Dream' in *Celtic Daily Prayer: Inspirational prayers and readings from the Northumbria Community* reads:

> *This world has become a world of broken dreams where dreamers are hard to find. Lord, be the gatherer of our dreams, you set the countless stars in place, and found room for each of them to shine. You listen for us in your heaven-bright hall.*[12]

How beautiful that God is the gatherer of our dreams, and that he waits and listens for them. How wonderful that we are assured that there is room for each of us to shine. For let us not forget that God is a dreamer too.

And as my Father dreams, so too will I dream, and I will wait for the dreams with my butterfly net, poised and ready as they come.

---

[12] *Celtic Daily Prayer: Inspirational prayers and readings from the Northumbria Community;* Harper Collins, 2000 (p.205).

3

For When We Don't Know
Where We're Going

35 DRUMMOND ROAD WAS THE PLACE THAT WE GREW UP IN, where we grew into ourselves. It was the first place that we felt was home, really home. It was the place we brought our newborn son home to. It was a safe place. In summer we would leave the back door open and in came the hum of cars on the streets nearby, the sound of children laughing as they went round and round on the roundabout over the road. Here is a poem that I wrote during that time.

Laundry

I stand amongst the whites in the yard,
still hung out to dry though it is getting dark.
I gather them in, the stone slabs rough and warm beneath my feet.
A hundred voices hum, a few doors slam, and
the yellow light of the kitchen spills out across the car park
where the boys from up the road do tricks on their skateboards,
the scrape of their wheels on the tarmac etches itself into my
    remembering.
Flotsam is carried up to these back doorsteps;
leaving unwanted tide lines:
things are heard that cannot be unheard.

Everyone knows what goes on, but still,
when they wake,
in the cold morning light,
the neighbours prowl around the edges
of their property,

guarding their lives,
their small secrets.

And I, mine, I suppose,
for behind this little blue gate,
and beyond this tatty yard,
within this see-through house,
as frail as a skeleton,
are all my life's treasures.

The smallness of that house was something that I treasured. It was cosy and safe, it wrapped tightly around us. But it was vulnerable too, so close to the street that we heard the footsteps and the heavy breaths as people strode down our road to the station; we heard drunken rows in the playground just over the road in the middle of the night.

Once there was a dog yapping outside the front and there was a man there lying face-down on the pavement. People came out of the woodwork then, to see if he was okay. People we'd never seen before, who said they lived down the road. Only two rooms from front to back, it was a see-through skeleton of a house too, as frail as an honesty seed head.

I had a sense that while we lived in that house, we had become giants and our feet and arms were poking out of the roof, out of the doors. We had outgrown it, that's for sure, but even now I miss it because it is a box of precious memories to me. And now I can't even remember the bad things; the bathroom that was falling to bits, and the overflow of stuff, bulging out from under the bed and the bottom of the wardrobe. Instead I remember the warm pine floor under my bare feet in the mornings; I remember Sam dragging a stool over to the window to watch the rubbish truck come past; I remember the sunlight filtering through the leaves of the tree, spreading golden flecks of light over the carpet in the lounge.

But even there, we felt the sense of *hiraeth,* to use a Welsh word with no direct English translation. The Oxford English Dictionary defines *hiraeth* as '*a homesickness for a home you cannot return to, or that never was*'. It is linked to nostalgia, the home that no longer exists because we have changed; but still we felt this gentle pull of our own country. There was the sense of a call, a homecoming. Almost like homing pigeons, we were restless because we were not in our homeland.

We had tried to put down roots in Surrey, we had lived there for ten years, we had made good friends but still felt rootless. I think a part of this was literally to do with not having a patch of land to sow into. We had a postage stamp of a yard that we couldn't really use. We had a bird feeder that no bird ever visited. It all had a sense of being temporary. We still felt that we were looking for something.

To use another Welsh concept, we were looking for our *cynefin,* a place of belonging to which we felt an intense spiritual connection.[13] We kept pressing it down, but it wouldn't go away. Natalie Goldberg, in *Writing Down the Bones,* talks of completing the circle in our lives. She says, *'It is very important to go home if you want your work to be whole,'*[14] not necessarily in the sense of having to return to live there, but in facing your roots and looking at them through new eyes.

Andre Gide says, *'One doesn't discover new lands without consenting to lose sight, for a very long time, of the shore,'*[15] and it is that sense of being adrift that is the scariest.

Because we don't always know what is coming. Psalm 119:129 says:

The unfolding of your words gives light; it gives understanding to the simple.[16]

To me this brings to mind the image of an origami bird, the paper being unfolded before me. It tells the story of our walk with God. Sometimes we want to see our lives mapped out before us, but it is God's wisdom that we cannot understand things that are beyond the place where we are now. Sometimes we need to wait and listen for his voice. The revelation comes in the unfolding, and in the stepping forward as we hear him.

So we felt a call, felt that something needed to change, and we prayed and waited for something to change and nothing did. We spent four years waiting for something to come up. We were pushing doors and none were opening. Sometimes, though, there has to be a catalyst; a moment of clarity causing you to say, enough is enough. When I fell unexpectedly

---

[13] Thomas Firbank talks about this concept in *I Bought a Mountain;* Hodder and Stoughton, 1988 [1940].

[14] Goldberg, Nathalie; *Writing Down the Bones;* Shambhala Publications, 2005 (p.237).

[15] Gide, Andre; *Les faux-monnayeurs [The Counterfeiters];* 1925.

[16] NIV.

pregnant with our third child, we took it as a sign to go. We put the house on the market and accepted an offer.

And then there was the waiting, and the questioning, because we didn't know what or where next. During this in-between time, God showed me the story of Abraham; that he didn't know where he was going but still he obeyed and went, that he had to get going and set out in faith:

> By faith Abraham, when he was called, obeyed by going out to a place which he was to receive for an inheritance; and he went out, not knowing where he was going.[17]

Sometimes it is the time for setting out, and that is the first step. This was our setting out from the shore. There was another image that spoke to me from my friend's photo reel on Facebook. It was a picture of her on holiday in the Alps; there was a great drift of snow and she was leaping into the air, two feet at once. You can't leap safely keeping one foot on safe ground. Leaping is an act of faith.

So there we were, risking safety, leaping wholly into the unknown. My husband handed his notice in and we trusted God as every detail of our house sale met with delays and complications. It took six months for the sale to go through, by which time I had had the baby. And before that, there was a whole summer of waiting.

---

[17] Hebrews 11:8 (NIV).

4

Roar

LET ME TELL YOU ABOUT THAT SUMMER. I WAS PREGNANT for the third time. We lived in a shoebox of a house, a beautiful God-provided house, but a shoebox nonetheless. We had a month of 30°C heat. I would take the kids out to the park in the morning, and we would have a good old splash in the paddling pool and be back home by 11, when the sun came out at its hottest. I'm so thankful that the house was cool. We had no garden, so I would close the curtains in the afternoon and put a DVD on for the children. I felt guilty, hot, tired, anxious, depressed. We had a futon which was too uncomfortable to sit on in my eight-month pregnant state so in the evenings I would lie on the bed, too tired to move. I worried that I would go into labour when there was no one to look after the children. Our bank balance was teetering on the edge of the abyss but we managed to keep going somehow. Everything that we lived felt like teeth-gritted hard work.

We had sold the house at Easter but everything, and I mean *everything*, went wrong with the sale. The crucial form got lost, the bank's head office in India didn't recognize the form, the solicitor went on holiday for two weeks, the buyers wanted to renegotiate the price, someone else went on holiday. We were desperate to move house, to be in a bigger place, to be nearer to family, to get Sam into a smaller preschool, to have the baby.

But every morning we woke up waiting. And in the end, all we had were questions. Why were we still there? Why was it such a squeeze? Why were we still waiting? It was exhausting and such a temptation to be stressed, but each time I just thought, *what can I actually do to change the situation? I can pray; I can place all my worries into the hands of the Father. I can say, my soul finds rest in God alone. I can take one day at a time.*

It was confusing because we knew it was the right thing to do and sometimes waiting is all just a part of the process. There are times in life when things make sense and times when we're floored by life, completely thrown. Something my mother said is that when you're young you think everything happens for a reason and when you get older you realise that nothing makes sense. Sometimes it feels like God is right there, leading us step by step, and sometimes it seems that he is remarkably absent.

We kept asking God why we were waiting, and I felt that God gave me this answer; he said, 'This is their safe space.' For our two young children, this house was all home meant to them. And although we were climbing the walls, they weren't. This home was all they knew. They were facing a lot of change and summer was just what they needed it to be. I felt that we just had to love them and give them time, because after the dust settled, everything would be different.

And then one day there was talk of an exchange. And then there was a phone call, there was a move date; there was an Internet search in the village we liked. There was one house. Just one that was available to rent. My parents went to see it and they said they could happily live there. And that was enough. There was a phone call. There was an agreement. We were standing in the hot and dusty playground, the one right opposite our house; the one that we said was our garden, that we walked across to after dinner, when it was bearable again to be outside. The one that we brought our son to when he was three days old, the one that we sat in drinking mugs of tea after dinner while we dreamed and schemed our life away.

And it did happen in the end; it all came together, and one bright morning in September when Benjamin was just two weeks old, we loaded our house into two vans and drove up the M40 to make a new home. Joel and I had dreamt about our new house and here's the list that we came up with: wood burner, fruit trees, garden, studio; and the thing I didn't even dare to ask for: a writing room. Our new house had every one of these things.

And what did I see on the first morning after the move, stumbling out of the car with Sam and Ivy, nervous and excited to begin at their new preschool? A huge rainbow filling the sky. Because God knew what time I would be dropping them off and his word to me in our new village, on the Abraham journey of our lives, was, 'I am faithful.' As I came out again, after having kissed and cuddled them in the doorway, it was already beginning to fade. It was just for then, just for that moment, just for us.

You see this life is a journey, and for me at least, I don't feel I have arrived yet. There is a sense in which we are at peace; there is a rest now where there was a striving. But these things don't last forever, and we don't know what is around the next corner, so we keep walking.

I wrote the poem below during that time of waiting. I was thinking about where I'd come from and where I was going. In my personal walk with God, one of the most helpful things has been to journal, to write things down, to dream on paper. It's so humbling and it builds faith to look back and see how God has answered the longings of your heart. So often we look at circumstance and things don't make any sense to us, but we can look up at God and have full trust in him that we are his and that he has got us in a safe place. Whatever happens, we are safe in him:

> *Let the beloved of the LORD rest secure in him, for he shields him all day long, and the one the LORD loves rests between his shoulders.[18]*

Guildford

We are thinking of saying goodbye to this place,
where the cobbles run down
and familiar faces sit at coffee shop windows.
The postman walks around the town,
and says good morning to me as though we are old friends,
and I wonder if he really remembers me,
because it was a good five years ago that I worked in the bookshop
and would sign for his parcels.

What have you given me, Guildford town?
Precious friends, a church (my second family),
three beautiful children: more than I could wish for.
But still we wonder if there is more,
if we are doing the right thing with our days.
What have you taken from me?
My friend Greg, my friend Jo,

---

[18] Deuteronomy 33:12 (NIV)

the ones I had a fondness for,
the ones who didn't come back to writing group,
the ones at work who I liked but who moved away
or did something new.
The ones that I no longer have an email address for,
the ones that I have lost in this world.

So where are we going? A new place but an old place;
a place that we remember in a thousand ways,
mostly because we don't know where else to go
(as if this world is small when it is big, so big!)
A place of spires, of cobbles, of rivers.
A place of water, of green, of markets and Tudor buildings.
Our little house on the market, we look at the estate agent's photos
and realise how bright, how beautiful it looks,
but we know too well how we roll around this tiny box
in frustration,
for it is good, but it is not enough.
'I want a good life for you,' I whisper to the children at night-time.
'I want a garden, space for you to run.'
A shelter from the strife of tongues, a safe place,
that is what I am looking for.
And what will I do that first morning when I am there,
in the new place?
Will I cry from relief, for this has been my prayer for four years?
(For the truth is that I cannot imagine somewhere
that is good enough.)
Will I regret what we have passed on, our precious pearl,
our manna; our bread for today?
For it was what we needed for so long, it was good.
And it is still good, but it is no longer ours.
So may it go to the right place, this gift.

Guildford, what have you honed and shaped in us?
A childish dependence, now spent and gone.
The dream, fresh still and green as the day it was born
and a lion-like roar to see it fulfilled.

This is the gift to me from my boy Sam today: his roar,
for it reminded me to go after things, to be loud in my quest,
to pursue them wholeheartedly and utterly
with everything that I am.

In *Listening to Your Life,* Frederick Buechner describes how the evidence of a plot in his life brought him to God.

> *You get married, a child is born or not born, in the middle of the night there is a knocking at the door, on the way home through the park you see a man feeding pigeons, all the tests come in negative and the doctor gives you back your life again: incident follows incident helter-skelter leading apparently nowhere, but then once in a while there is the suggestion of purpose, meaning, direction, the suggestion of plot, the suggestion that, however clumsily, your life is trying to tell you something, take you somewhere.*[19]

Like Buechner, I have seen the evidence of plot in my life. There is a story that is being built, one of God at work in our lives. There are nudges, whispers that have caused great change. The story that is being written is for telling and re-telling.

And in the midst of this topsy-turvy plot, where nothing seems to make sense, if we pour out our heart to God, it can make things clearer, difficult trials can somehow sit right with our souls. Instead of the confusion, two things remain: 1) this is what I'm struggling with; and 2) this is what you have said. A verse that was really encouraging to me in this time spoke of Abraham believing God's word over what he saw. What faith!

> *Without weakening in his faith, he faced the fact that his body was as good as dead – since he was about 100 years old – and that Sarah's womb was also dead. Yet he did not waver through unbelief regarding the promise of God but was fully persuaded that God had the power to do what he had promised.*[20]

---

[19] Buechner, Frederick; *Listening to Your Life;* Harper Collins, 1992 (p.82).
[20] Romans 4:19,20 (NIV)

I realised as I wrote this poem that our time in Guildford had birthed in us our roar, the desires of our heart, the calling on our lives to write, to make music, and that in all the struggle and winding paths was the thread of faithfulness, of God pulling us onward. *This is what I'm growing in you,* he said. *The trials make you more desperate for it, and the passion that will be birthed in this time is no bad thing.*

5

How I Write

THIS IS HOW IT IS THEN, THE STRUGGLE FOR SOLITUDE, FOR creativity, after the move. I take the children to school and preschool, and afterwards I walk back home and put Benjamin down for a nap. As he settles, I walk downstairs and boil the kettle. I watch the cloud of steam rise and I think about what I am going to write that day. I dream of these characters and people that I will revisit, that I will spend time with. I plug my phone in downstairs so it will not distract me. I make a strong cup of tea with half a sugar and a good splosh of milk. I carry it upstairs to my writing room and close the door behind me. I leave the washing up, the laundry, the floor that could do with a mop, the toys scattered all over the place. There isn't enough time to worry about these things; my good friend Jo always told me that. There are more important things than a tidy house. I am blessed to have a room to myself, I know that much. It is such a precious thing. I think back to the last house, where the desk was shoved in the corner with the Moses basket on top. My workspace was wherever I could make it, wherever I perched with my laptop on my knee. But life with young children is full of interruptions, and at least here I know that I can walk in, close the door and find everything just as I left it; hideously messy but just as it was.

I look out of the window, down the garden towards the shed. The leaves have turned yellow and have fallen like a halo around the base of the tree. I sit down and begin searching for my thought trails, leafing through the pieces of paper. I find where I was up to; it takes a few minutes to settle. I am always leaving things in the middle. There are telephones that ring, children that wake up, children that need to be collected from preschool. I write down two quotes and pin them up. I close the books that I was reading from yesterday. I look at my to-do list and add a few more things that I can think of. In fact, most days I start a new one. I see no problem with this, it is the way my brain works. If I have written it down, I don't need to worry about it anymore. Even if I write the same thing over and over it is OK, because it reinforces in my mind what needs to be done.

I am a great believer in my crowd of witnesses that cheers me on, the words of writers that resonate with me. Sometimes it seems that the truth they have found sounds a lot like the truth I have found. I recently came across what I take to be my mandate for now. For me, this sums up better than anything else the heart of why I am doing what I do. There is a speechlessness that comes sometimes when you read something that captures so perfectly what you had hoped to say, or not even that, something that was in your heart but something that you hadn't yet dreamt of saying. Reading anything by Marilynne Robinson usually sets this off within me. But my mantra comes from Frederick Buechner's *Listening to Your Life;* this is what I long to do with my writing:

> *Let him use [words] to set us dreaming as well as thinking, to stir in us intuitions and longings that we starve for without knowing that we starve.*[21]

Feeding people who don't know that they are hungry, or something like that.

There is a bookshelf, too, just above my desk and it is full of all the things I am reading about or thinking about right now. There is always a shelf rammed full, with more books lying sideways on top. There is so much to read but having it right there reminds me of what I have been thinking about. It is a bit like a to-do list in books. I am a visual person and I like to know that I can lay my hand to any book that I have been thinking about (in fact, it sets me off in a bit of a panic if I can't find a certain book and is a sure-fire way for me to waste half an hour searching).

I open my file called Junk. This is equivalent to my morning pages, as described in Julia Cameron's *The Artist's Way.* This is where I write down what I am feeling, what is preoccupying my mind and I let it all go in a river and there I am free; it doesn't matter what I write (it is called Junk, after all).

Then, when I am ready, I get on with it; I write and brainstorm, encouraged by this cheer from my crowd of witnesses, this comfy chair, this good strong tea, to write. If I am discouraged, I look up and sigh,

---

[21] Buechner, Frederick; *Listening to Your Life;* Harper Collins, 1992 (p.284).

and then I find a jewel and get back on with it. Here's one from Virginia Woolf that is blu-tacked up in front of me as I write:

> *So long as you write what you wish to write that is all that matters, and whether it matters for ages or only for hours, nobody can say. But to sacrifice a hair of the head of your vision, a shade of its colour is the most abject treachery.*[22]

I hold this to be true for me. Better to be true to yourself than to create for someone else. Sometimes, if it is in the evening, I light a candle, I make it holy. I shut the door so there is time; I indulge myself in the things that I love. I allow myself to drift, *'to let the line of thought dip deep into the stream'*[23].

Sometimes I walk out of the room having accomplished absolutely nothing but there is just the feeling that there was something important, something vital that I was getting on with. And for now, that is okay.

Monday

It is always on a Monday
that the shores of our hope rise.
On this day, we believe in these dreams of ours;
we sit at our life's tapestry and sew.
It is this morning that we know there is work to be done.
It is this morning that we pack the children off to preschool
and there is a blissful silence in the house,
one that is punctuated only by the happy drone
of a lawnmower outside the window,
and the heavy, sleepy breaths of Benjamin.
Soon he will be a rambunctious crawler,
shunning sleep in the morning,
but just for now, it works,
and just for now, Monday is a safe shore.
I close the door after these few treasured hours,
leaving the things as they are,
the mess on the desk,

---

[22] Woolf, Virginia; *A Room of One's Own;* Penguin, 2000 [1920] (p.96).
[23] *Ibid.* (p.98).

the books strewn all around me
on the futon because I know that
next time I sneak away
to this private place,
it will all be just as I left it.

6

For When We Don't Know
What Is Coming

SO THERE WE WERE, IN THE WILDS OF SHROPSHIRE, WITH A two-week-old baby and two preschoolers, and everything was new. My husband was beginning to concentrate on his music full-time, and the two eldest children had just started in a new preschool. There was time for the dust to settle. But I still had a nagging feeling that something was wrong. It felt as if there was a sadness in the house so we prayed in each room. But I still felt vulnerable, because I had left my home, my safe space, and come to this new place that was wonderful but big and full of unfamiliar curtains and smells. I was craving somewhere to hibernate with my newborn and I didn't feel safe yet, but we had to hit the ground running. Looking back, it felt like we were waiting for something.

And then just four weeks after we moved, our daughter Ivy was diagnosed with Type I diabetes. We didn't understand how our confident, beautiful, articulate two-year-old daughter who had never even been to the doctor suddenly had this thing in her that was broken and that would never go back to normal. They told us she would have to have four injections and multiple blood tests every day for the rest of her life. And straight away, that first night when she had to go to hospital with her daddy, and I was sat in the house in the dark with the boys in their beds, I prayed for healing. I put her into the hands of her heavenly Father and I said, *she is yours, take care of her.* Because I was her mother and I was utterly helpless to look after her. But also, because there was nothing else I could do. So I slept (or mostly not slept) in the bed by myself, an uncertain four-year-old Sam coming to join me in the night because he was unused to sleeping in the bedroom without his sister.

And it was like learning to walk again. I remember walking out of the children's ward in the October sunshine thinking that I felt more scared than when we had walked out of hospital with our firstborn son. We felt that we didn't know how to look after her, this treasure, this joyful girl. But we learnt again. And also, God gave us a new love for her, a deeper love for her, a new realisation of how precious she is to us, and he gave us the shining light of his hope for her, because we will never give up hope for her healing. We kept coming back to this verse in those first few days:

> May the God of all hope fill you with all joy and peace as you trust in him and may you overflow with hope by the power of the Holy Spirit.[24]

A few weeks later, as I was pouring out my heart to my Father, he whispered back, 'Nothing can take away how safe she is in me.' And that is what I cling to daily; that she is safe with her God and that he numbers the days of her life. And I pray that he will give her a supernatural grace to deal with her injections and a double portion of joy.

Because really, we do not know what is coming, none of us know what is around the corner, but a special grace comes from the Father for when we cannot cope, and those that are the smallest among us often have brave and unknown ways of dealing with hard things. She is a fearless girl; she takes it all in her stride; she astounds me daily.

It brings to mind a May morning a year or two ago when I was wandering around RHS Wisley near where we used to live. The blossoms were out and in the Wild Garden the paths wove around and opened out into secret little places where there would be the most lavish and beautiful blooms, deep pink and white and purple and yellow. It was extravagantly beautiful; breathtaking. And I felt that God said to me then, 'This is what life is like. It is not a straight path, and you do not know what is coming around the corner. But some things become even more beautiful when they are unexpected. This is the surprise of joy. They are even more beautiful because you did not see them coming.' There are good things, all the time there are good things, and there are hard things too.

And so we thank you, Father, for the joy in this life, and we thank you that although we do not understand the pain, you are with us in it. Thank you that when we pass through the waters you will be with us,

---

[24] Romans 15:13 (NIV).

when we pass through the rivers they will not sweep over us, and when we walk through the fire we will not be burned.[25]

Trembling Heart

I held you to me on the bed and smelt your hair, felt your lightness,
as your father bustled in the darkness for your favourite things.
We had been to the doctor's that afternoon and he rang
as we were driving home
to the clear light, where the town stopped and the hills began.

I saw the phone number flash up on the screen and I knew
it was serious.
Something far down in me had sensed that it wasn't going to
go away,
but I wasn't prepared to listen to that, wasn't ready to have you
    here like this,
breathing against me like a baby bird.

Your father had brought you home from the hospital.
It was late at night and he had to take you back again.
His face was white, and he wasn't thinking straight.
And I held you on the bed thinking, this is the last time;
the last time that you are mine,
that you do not have diabetes,
that everything is OK.

I kissed you goodbye and sent you off
to that white unforgiving hospital
while I stayed home for the baby,
but I remember holding you on that bed.

The drum of my heart was loud,
and I was so small in your arms
and all I had left was this helplessness.

---

[25] See Isaiah 43:1,2 (NIV).

Type I

Walking out of hospital
on a cold but bright day,
clutching armfuls of her silly things;
Mr. Carrot and Mr. Strawberry,
her walking ahead of us
all jolly and bright,
singing even
in the October dusk,
and us following behind,
tearful and uncertain.
The bag of drugs they give us
to take home is almost as big as she is
and I feel more afraid than I did
when our firstborn came home,
swaddled with blankets and worry,
as the silver Sharan carried him.

7

The Ways in Which We Are Like Pots

THERE IS A JAPANESE WORD *KINTSUJUROI* WHICH MEANS TO repair with gold. If a pot gets broken, it is not thrown away but is renewed. The beauty is not found in the perfection of the object but in its journey; it becomes more beautiful for having been broken and repaired. Through this journey something of heaven can be shown. In his letter to the Corinthians, the apostle Paul says:

> *We have this treasure in jars of clay to show that this all-surpassing power is from God and not from us.*[26]

It was from a cracked pot that pure nard was poured out to anoint the King,[27] and it was only by breaking the pot that this fragrance could be released.

I love the fact that God's ways are not our ways and that the eternal mysteries of God are something that we keep learning over and over. They don't naturally make sense to us, we can't see them coming. In the world, we say we can't give what we don't have. We say we're broken; we're not ready to be used. But in God's kingdom, there is a new way; we give and it is given to us. There is an inflow and an overflow. There is no lack. We are rich in him and he will meet our needs:

> *Now he who supplies seed to the sower and bread for food will also supply and increase your store of seed and will enlarge the harvest of your righteousness. You will be enriched in every way so that you can be generous on every occasion, and through us your generosity will result in thanksgiving to God.*[28]

---

[26] 2 Corinthians 4:7 (NIV).
[27] See Mark 14:3-9.
[28] 2 Corinthians 9:10,11 (NIV)

As we pour out to him, he pours into us. It is a river, a flow of fresh water, freshly received, freshly given. The Bible tells us to...

> ...*give and it will be given to you. A good measure, pressed down, shaken together and running over will be poured into your lap. For with the measure you use, it will be measured to you.*[29]

I love these pictures of overflow; these are not scant measures, but more than enough, abundantly enough:

> ...*my cup overflows.*[30]

Once this flow is opened, it will bring refreshing to others. Let's not hold back our love because we think there won't be enough left for us, or because we think we're too broken to be any good; that is the world's way. If we feel that we are empty or don't have enough, then perhaps it is a gentle nudge that we need to come and sit at the Father's feet for a while. May Sarton, an American writer, spoke of this flow of life regarding her creativity; she wrote that:

> *There is only one real deprivation [...] and that is not to be able to give one's gift to those one loves most. [...] The gift turned inward, unable to be given, becomes a heavy burden, even sometimes a kind of poison. It is as though the flow of life were backed up.*[31]

I cannot emphasise enough how true this has been in my life. Releasing your creations gives you the headspace to move on to the next thing. We cannot continue on the journey if we are stultified.

I think that the flow of life that Sarton speaks of can be seen to be this life with Christ, lavish, overflowing and ever-sustaining. May we open up the channels to let out the overflow. May we press in to know more of his abundance. May we always be ready to give of ourselves because with him the well will never run dry.

It is okay to be broken! We are living in jars of clay, that's how he made us. Think of the pot, smashed to bits and lovingly repaired by the master with gold. These cracks or pressure points are where God can

---

[29] Luke 6:38 (NIV).
[30] Psalm 23:5 (NIV).
[31] Sarton, May; *Journal of a Solitude;* Norton, 1973 (p.168).

shine through, where there is nothing left of us but heavenly gold. Our wounds and times of great pain can be transformed into memories of great love. I remember a time as a teenager when I broke up with a boyfriend and I felt so broken, rejected and hurt that I came to God every day and listened to a song called *Hungry* written by Kathryn Scott. The lyrics say: *'Hungry, I come to you for I know you satisfy. I am weary but I know your touch restores my life,'* and I literally felt like God was sustaining my life. I felt that I wouldn't be able to get through the day without being near to my Father God. Now when I think back, instead of remembering that time as one of great pain, I remember it as one that was vulnerable but full of a growing awareness of my Father God's love for me.

Lewis Hyde, in *The Gift,* a fascinating book about gift exchange and creativity, notes that in cultures with a gift economy…

> *…when a gift is used, it is not used up. Quite the opposite in fact: the gift that is not used will be lost, while the one that is passed along remains abundant.*[32]

There is something in the giving away that keeps it alive. Jesus spoke of this renewing water that is not used up but increased when he spoke to the woman at the well:

> *Everyone who drinks of this water will thirst again; but whoever drinks the water I give them will never thirst. Indeed, the water I give them will become in them a spring of water welling up to eternal life.*[33]

This is how it works in the topsy-turvy kingdom of heaven: we give when we don't have and he uses us even when we're broken.

The following poem is about our creativity, that precious seed within us that we long to come to fruition. It speaks of the struggle of the seed within us to be born, that our treasure is sometimes hidden, or buried within, but God is committed to our character and to our giftings. He has planted desires within us and longs, as we do, to see these come to fruition. Looking at the Amplified translation, it is clear how much God longs for us to walk in the good plans that he has for us, to be who he made us to be; and for a creator, what we create is who we are.

---

[32] Hyde, Lewis; *The Gift;* Canongate, 2006 [1983] (p.21).
[33] John 4:13,14 (NASB).

For we are His workmanship [His own master work, a work of art], created in Christ Jesus [reborn from above – spiritually transformed, renewed, ready to be used] for good works, which God prepared [for us] beforehand [taking paths which He set], so that we would walk in them [living the good life which He prearranged and made ready for us].[34]

How he longs for us to walk in these good plans that he has laid for us!

Even Still

As when
it seems that there is nothing left,
nothing but a shred of yourself.
Like a flag on a hilltop,
bare and waiting.

As when the wind comes rushing through,
with the train going by
at the station,
the hot fumes pushed
into your face like a bad kiss:
a dirty kick from life that says
even though.
Even though you do all of this;
you stand here on this
dull, grey
platform,
and you jostle amongst the
elbows and shoulders of strangers.
Even though your mouth tastes of strong coffee
and you have not quite woken fully,
and your mind is thinking back to last night,
to those words that you said.

---

[34] Ephesians 2:28 (AMP).

Even though, you will come
from your shell, your carapace today;
you will be pushed out of hiding by this life.
That thing that you carry,
your burden, your heart-shaped weight
will come out
and show itself,
shy and beautiful pearl
that it is,
or might be,
given half a chance.

No matter how you feel,
it is rising.

There is no apology:
you will be blown through,
turned inside out like glass,
molten, taking shape,
or a lump of dough in the baker's hands,
kneaded until ready,
broken until supple,
like a flag in the wind,
ragged and waiting.

It will not be crushed
by this sometimes hard and cruel life.
The smouldering wick will not be snuffed out,
but the faint spark of grace will come,
and what you have
will be galvanised in your hands.

For there, hidden behind weary eyes,
beyond the drudge of work,
the weight of worry
is a bright light.

And it will come through, even still,
as the player in the pit
tightens his reed in place,
presses his lips to the mouthpiece and blows,
and the clear notes come through
as you never thought they might,
from two inches of reed,
and a piece
of black wood.

If May Sarton's words resonate with you, then can I challenge you to create something and to give it away? Make a card, write a poem, compose a piece of music and record it on to CD, choreograph a dance, take a photo, print it out and give it away. Start to live in your giftings. I really believe that God has set these gifts within you and me to set the world on fire, and by 'the world', I mean whomever you see, your family, your friends. It may be a big circle; it may be small. But that is not your responsibility. Your responsibility is to hone your giftings and to release them into the world, and then to stand back and see what happens.

8

This Is the Year of Loving Myself More

'THIS IS THE YEAR OF LOVING MYSELF MORE.' THE PHRASE came to me a couple of days ago and hasn't left. It came as a grace antidote to all the New Year's resolutions that I had miserably failed at keeping and since shelved. What came up was the feeling that my soul knew what it wanted to be doing but that I wasn't listening to myself.

Living with two young children on a tight budget in the South East of England had meant negating myself and my desires for quite a while. I was mean with myself. 'I don't need it' was my mantra and mostly I wouldn't buy it, whatever it was. I was well used to looking jealously into coffee shop windows where people were sitting by themselves *reading,* an indulgence that I rarely allowed myself. 'It's alright for them,' I would huff, burning with jealousy. There were things that I wanted to pursue – an art course, learning book arts, going on a writing retreat, learning to crochet, even buying a new novel; in short, indulging in my creativity – but each time I would cut myself off in my tracks, asking, 'Is it essential?' and then mostly deciding against it.

I'm not denying that with young children it is a juggle, but to keep supressing the creative pursuit in ourselves is no noble thing. Julia Cameron, in the quite wonderful *Artist's Way,* says:

> *Many of us have made a virtue out of deprivation. [...] We strive to be good, to be nice, to be helpful, to be unselfish. [...] But what we really want is to be left alone. When we can't get others to leave us alone, we eventually abandon ourselves. To others, we may look like we're there. We may act like we're there. But our true self has gone to ground.*[35]

---

[35] Cameron, Julia; *The Artist's Way;* Jeremy P. Tarcher / Putnam, 2002 [1992] (p.98).

And today I encourage you: don't let yourself go to ground! The world needs people that are on fire with life and who know what they were born to do. Julia Cameron recommends 'artist dates' which are a way to value your gifting and the things that God made you to love. Go to an art gallery, she says, go for a crisp autumn walk. Even if (especially if) you have young children, persuade a friend or a partner to take them off your hands just for a little while so you can do something that will make you feel valued for who you are with all your idiosyncrasies and foibles, something that will make you feel like *you* again.

So there I was, just the other day, standing in the craft shop with my two-year-old and my four-month-old, feeling dizzy from the rush of desires that suddenly swept over me. Knowing that I had three small children and no time but that I wanted to write, to read, to learn cross-stitch, to make scrapbooks about my children. I suddenly felt a sense of sadness at all that I so wanted to do and felt I didn't have the time for.

But then a little voice said, 'But there is time. There is one day at a time; there is the gentle unfolding of life.' And there and then I allowed myself the luxury. I bought myself some beautiful paper and some ribbons and I thought, *this is the year of loving myself more.*

My husband and I did *The Marriage Course* together a few years ago and they said, carve out time for yourselves, go on dates together; but we didn't live near family to get babysitters, so we thought, *nice advice but it won't work for us.* But as we bickered over dinner recently in front of our four-year-old son, I realised that being kind to my marriage will bless our home and it will bless our son. The relationship between my husband and me is the foundation of our home, and if we neglect the foundations, it won't be long before everything else starts to crumble. There are certain things we cannot do at this stage in our family life, but there are also the things that we can do. We can choose to bless each other. We can turn off the phones, TVs and PCs and spend time together. We can cook dinner together. We can look each other in the eye when we talk; we can share a bottle of wine in the evening. This is the year of loving our marriage more.

Sometimes I am plagued by the thought that writing, my great love, is frivolous, that it is an added extra to my life, that it doesn't need looking after, but it is what I keep coming back to. There is something that won't let me put it down. It is a part of me. And although I may not be changing the world, my job is to see truth, to see humanity, to see beauty, to put it down on the page. And what does God think of my vocation? Well, he is the one who gave it to me, after all. I was looking recently at the parable of the talents where the servant says, *'Sir, here is your mina; I have kept it laid away in a piece of cloth. I was afraid of you.'* [36] And I thought, 'Far be it from me to bury what God has given to me in the ground.' If I bury what he has put in me in favour of the recognition and the praise of man, of an unwanted career, I do not trust his goodness to me. This is the year of loving my writing more too.

So this coming year, invest in what God has given you, don't bury it away. Honour him by honouring the gifting that is within you. Listen to yourself, like yourself. Be kind to yourself. Follow the whims of your heart, the yearnings of your soul. Invest in the things that are important – your friendships, your marriage, your gifting.

> *Every good thing given and every perfect gift is from above, coming down from the Father of lights, with whom there is no variation or shifting shadow.* [37]

Because how can you show others that your Father God is a lavish and generous father if you do not love yourself?

---

[36] Luke 19:21 (NIV).
[37] James 1:17 (NASB).

9

Incorruptible Seed

WHAT IF THERE WERE A PLACE IN YOU THAT WAS PURE heaven? What if you could create works of art that no one had seen before? What if you had the power in you to release heaven on earth? What if you had unclouded access to the heart of God? The Bible says that we have been...

> ...born again, not of corruptible seed, but of incorruptible, by the word of God, which lives and abides forever.[38]

I imagine this seed within us to be solid silver or gold. How amazing that right at the heart of us, there is something of heaven. And through Jesus, we do have access to the throne! It says in Hebrews:

> Seeing then that we have a great high priest, [...] Let us come boldly unto the throne of grace, that we may obtain mercy, and find grace to help in time of need.[39]

We may come boldly!

So come, sit, rest. Virginia Woolf encouraged writers to 'let the line of thought dip deep into the stream'[40]. And isn't this stream the water of life, the Holy Spirit's refreshing? The challenge is to silence the clamour of our days, to find that still small voice of God, to bring our creativity to him each day, to tap into the seam of gold that runs through us. I say amen to heavenly downloads. Creative practitioners, whether professing to have a faith or not, often credit the eternal, or at least something other than themselves, for the inspiration that comes to them. Lewis Hyde in *The Gift* states:

---

[38] 1 Peter 1:23 (KJV).
[39] Hebrews 4:16 (KJV).
[40] Woolf, V.; *A Room of One's Own;* Penguin, 2000 [1929] (p.63).

The gifted man is not himself [...] until he has become the steward of wealth which appears from beyond his realm of influence and which, once it has come to him, he must constantly disburse. [...] We are sojourners with our gifts, not their owners; even our creations – especially our creations do not belong to us. As Gary Snyder says, 'You get a good poem and you don't know where it came from. "Did I say that?" And so all you feel is; you feel humility and you feel gratitude.' Spiritually, you can't be much poorer than gifted.[41]

How wonderful, this humility, this acknowledgement of the holy, of the creative force that is at work outside our own. In the UK, houses are given a blue plaque if someone famous has lived there. A while ago, I was daydreaming and thought, wouldn't it be wonderful to have plaques that said this is where this person was inspired to create this work of art, or this is where this person met God?

There is a feeling of these works, being there in the air around us: poems, symphonies, plays, works of art that are longing to come into being. For God can use us, and he can use our works of art in unimaginable ways. So how do we still the noise and listen for these treasures?

A large part is learning to find our voice. This is not just for writers. Painters, composers, dancers all need to find their authentic voice, one that is not a replica of something else that they have seen, but something that comes from deep within. To find our voice, we need to give ourselves time. In *The Artist's Way,* Julia Cameron wisely warns:

Competition lies at the root of much creative blockage. As Artists, we must go within. We must attend to what it is our inner guidance is nudging us toward.[42]

It's all too easy in our world of social media to share too much too quickly and to seek validation when a work is not yet finished. It's almost like we need to go into hiding for a while, to stop listening to all the voices until we have mined out the gold from our lives, until we have

---

[41] Hyde, Lewis; *The Gift;* Canongate, 2006 [1983] (p.282).

[42] Cameron, Julia; *The Artist's Way;* Jeremy P. Tarcher / Putnam, 2002 [1992] (p.173).

found what we have been waiting to say. Virginia Woolf gives you permission to wander until you have found it:

> *Literature is no one's private ground. Let us trespass freely and fearlessly and find our way for ourselves.*[43]

I agree here that wandering is the way to find your voice. Read, taste, see, and when you find something that resonates with you, then take note of it. Finding your voice is about starting out on the journey. In *Quiet,* Susan Cain makes the point about introverts:

> *Being relatively unmotivated by rewards gives you incalculable power to go your own way. It's up to you to use that independence to good effect.*[44]

This is good advice for all creatives, introverts or not. Arvo Pärt, the Latvian composer, famously went into retreat for seven years and didn't compose a single piece, for he was learning and he was listening. It's tempting to rush, but some things take time. Louise Erdrich, a novelist, speaks of her journals:

> *I have always kept notebooks – I have an obsessive devotion to them – and I go back to them over and over. They are my compost pile of ideas. Any scrap goes in and after a while I'll get a handful of earth.*[45]

It is this maturing, this sifting through of ideas and experience that can at last be distilled into something else, a thought, a feeling. And it takes time.

Julia Cameron says:

> *Let reviewers concern themselves with what is in and what is not. Let us concern ourselves first and foremost with what is in us that is struggling to be born.*[46]

You are the only one who can communicate your message to the world so give it time to be born. Don't rush.

---

[43] Woolf, V.; *A Room of One's Own;* Penguin, 2000 [1929] (p.63).
[44] Cain, Susan; *Quiet;* Penguin, 2012 (p.173).
[45] Interview with Louise Erdrich; 'Art of Fiction 208'; *The Paris Review.*
[46] Cameron, Julia; *The Artist's Way;* Jeremy P. Tarcher / Putnam, 2002 [1992] (p.173).

There is a great part of mystery in all of this: there is something telling us how to live, where to go next, who we are. We wonder how can we not know who we are? But I, for one, believe in the mystery, and I love the mystery. I am too complicated for myself to work out, but also there is space then for the great dance of the eternal and the temporal, the love relationship of a father with his children. We need to follow the trails of breadcrumbs. Do you ever feel that you are on to something? Follow that thing that you are on to. Frederick Buechner identifies our tears as a powerful communicator to us:

> *...they are not only telling you something about the secret of who you are, but more often than not, God is speaking to you through them of the mystery of where you have come from and is summoning you to where, if your soul is saved, you should go next.*[47]

So how can we follow this trail of breadcrumbs, to know our true selves? Here are some practical ideas:

- Pay attention to the whims of your heart – what interests you? I have a book on Labrador sat on my shelf that I love – for some reason, the icy regions of the north fascinate me. List five things that you have wanted to do but have never got around to doing. Now make some practical steps to go and do one of those things.

- Seamus Heaney, the Irish poet says this about finding our voice:

> *How then do you find it? In practice, you hear it coming from somebody else, you hear something in another writer that flows in through your ear and enters the echo chamber of your heart and delights your whole nervous system in such a way that your reaction will be, 'Ah I wish I had said that, in that particular way.' [...] This other writer, in fact, has spoken something essential to you, something you recognise instinctively as a true sounding of aspects of yourself and your experience and your first steps as a writer will be to imitate, consciously or unconsciously, those sounds that flowed in, that in-fluence.*[48]

---

[47] Buechner, Frederick; *Listening to Your Life;* Harper Collins, 1992 (p.237).
[48] Heaney, Seamus; *Finders Keepers;* Faber and Faber, 2002 (p.16).

Sometimes I read something and think, *I could have written that,* or, even better, that I could never have imagined a thought so beautiful but it resonates deeply with me. I picked up a book of poetry in a bookshop recently and it gave me goosebumps. It was so beautiful and the writing so true to me that it produced a physical reaction. Notice what provokes this reaction in you. Write it down; gather the clues to who you are.

- Pay attention to your other emotions too: What makes you cry? What brings you joy? What makes you angry?

- Don't stop growing. Don't settle. Don't build your house in the wrong place. Think of Abraham setting out on his journey:

By faith Abraham, when called to go to a place he would later receive as his inheritance, obeyed and went, even though he did not know where he was going. By faith he made his home in the promised land like a stranger in a foreign country; he lived in tents, as did Isaac and Jacob, who were heirs with him of the same promise. For he was looking forward to the city with foundations [the heavenly Jerusalem, symbolic of the presence of God], whose architect and builder is God.[49]

- Keep notebooks. Write your heart cries, read them over. Notice the ground that you are uncovering. Julia Cameron speaks marvellously of morning pages:

It is impossible to write morning pages for any extended period of time without coming into contact with an unexpected inner power [...] the pages are a pathway to a strong and clear sense of self. They are a trail that we follow into our own interior, where we meet both our own creativity and our creator. Morning pages map our terra incognita. Without them, our dreams may remain terra incognita.[50]

I heard the novelist Jackie Kay speaking once. She said to realise that as a writer, you have ground that you will keep going over and over. There are things in your soul that need to get out and

---

[49] Hebrews 11:8 (NIV).
[50] Cameron, Julia; *The Artist's Way;* Jeremy P. Tarcher / Putnam, 2002 [1992] (pp.14-15).

sometimes you will come out with painting after painting that speaks of the same theme. These are the themes of your life and that is OK. Let them come out.

10

Living in the Moment

YOU KNOW THOSE QUOTES THAT YOU CARRY AROUND WITH you that remind you how to live? One of mine, from my teenage years when I daydreamed and pinned quotes up on my wall, was this:

The only thing you ever really own is the instant that you are living in.

I don't even know where this quote comes from, but I remember repeating it to myself as I was growing up. It's so true though, isn't it? We try to hold on to other things, but we just can't.

Having small children brings this sense of 'now' home. Some days you ache for them to be older, to be in school, for them not to need you to get them a drink, change their nappy, spoon feed them. But it goes so fast. All I have of my children when they were very young are baby photos and a few videos shot on my mobile. But when I watch them back, I almost feel burdened with the sadness that it has all gone. I can't even remember the sound of my daughter's voice when she was that small. I feel like I want to archive it all, to keep it all. But in reality, you can't keep it. There are photos and there are memories. Sometimes we look at an old photo and we have a degree of the memory, but part of the wistfulness comes from the fact that you can never have that moment again, that same smell, that same emotion. Today, more than ever we want to document what happens. We want to capture things that are vanishing and though our technology lets us, it is a futile attempt. Apparently, these days we take more than 380 billion photos a year. Every two minutes we take more pictures than were taken in the whole of the 1800s.[51]

---

[51] See *www.buzzfeed.com/hunterschwarz/how-many-photos-have-been-taken-ever-6zgv#.kd9ByN1P1.*

When I was in my twenties, I felt like nothing really changed. I may have changed job, or moved to a new flat, but nothing so life-changing as the last six years. And to think that six-and-a-bit years ago there was just my husband and me muddling through life. Now there are five of us and everything is a bit louder.

So let us live fully, completely drenched in this thing called life. Frederick Buechner, an American writer and minister, puts it like this:

> *You are seeing everything for the last time and everything you see is gilded with goodbyes. The child's hand like a starfish on the pillow, your hand on the doorknob. [...] And today now everything will pass because it is the last day. For the last time you are seeing this rain fall and in your mind that snow, this child asleep, this cat. [...] All the unkept promises if they are ever to be kept have to be kept today. All the unspoken words if you do not speak them today will never be spoken. The people, the ones who you love and the ones who bore you to death; all the life you have in you to live with them, if you do not live it with them today will never be lived. It is the first day because it has never been before and the last day because it will never be again. Be alive if you can all through this day today of your life. What's to be done? What's to be done? Follow your feet. Put on the coffee. Start the orange juice, the bacon, the toast. Then go wake up your children and your wife. Think about the work of your hands, the book that of all conceivable things you have chosen to add to the world's pain. Live in the needs of the day.*[52]

How freeing and how humbling, that this is all there is. Young children already know this and they live fully, overflowing with emotion, full of tears and laughter. Whatever they feel, it has to do with 'now'. So let's be thankful for the now, however difficult, tiring or hard it may be.

And isn't it the same with these creative burdens that we carry with us, that we hide away thinking, *another day, another day...*? Because really, all there is, is this day. And sometimes you need a moment where you think, *what does it matter what anyone thinks?* Where you think as I have thought, 'Far be it from me to bury what you have given me.' Where you think it is better to try than to do nothing at all.

---

[52] Buechner, Frederick; *Listening to Your Life;* Harper Collins, 1992 (p.88).

I love the story of Rabbi Zusya who lived in the 1700's. He said:

When I get to the heavenly court, God will not ask me, 'Why weren't you Moses?' Rather he will ask me, 'Why were you not Zusya?'

It is so easy to compare ourselves to others, but it can really throw us off track and be discouraging. I can put it no better than Paul in his letter to the Galatians:

Make a careful exploration of who you are and the work you have been given and then sink yourself into that. Don't be impressed with yourself. Don't compare yourself to others. Each of you must take responsibility for doing the creative best you can with your own life.[53]

So have a think and take stock. Do you keep putting off creativity? What are you waiting for? Remember that today is all there is. Is there one small thing you can do today? Not tomorrow, but today. Take a step towards your dream, however small. And then keep taking steps. This is the only way you are going to get there, after all.

---

[53] Galatians 6:4-5 (MSG).

11

Circles

How it has come to this,
that we should dance, our bodies whirling around,
our hands turning the planet as we spin?
That we should laugh out loud past midnight,
and share the mutterings of our disbelief under stale breath?
That one night, up at the house,
with the curtains drawn and all the lights on,
we should stay up dancing?

We have been waiting so long for this, and now
our daughter has given birth to a child.
A little boy, they say.
That's why.

And so we make midnight coffee,
and plan what to say when we first see him.
We pack our bags to be off at first light,
and joke about whose nose he will have, whose eyes,

Our voices waver and crack like reeds at the thought of it,
and afterwards we sit,
holding each other's hands,
to steady ourselves.

LIFE GOES IN CIRCLES. WE BUILD ON WHAT HAS BEEN BEFORE,
we grow up, become like our parents, some of us have children, we grow
old, we become dependent again. We do the same things year in, year

out; we live through all the summers and winters in the rhythms of this lovely old planet.

As creatives, we live with our eyes wide open, we really see the world for all its glory and brokenness, but I believe that there is a creative legacy behind us and we have the permission to tap into that and to take it forward. Picture a wave swelling behind you, the weight and thrust of all the pictures of heaven that others have seen and revealed on earth. Our purpose as creatives is to listen for the gold of the kingdom of heaven and sow the seeds of it over the earth. What a joy, what a privilege, to be used by our Father.

> *Those who sow in tears shall reap with joyful shouting. He who goes to and fro weeping, carrying his bag of seed, shall indeed come again with a shout of joy, bringing his sheaves with him.*[54]

This Psalm talks about these circles; one sows, another reaps, we are building something, some marvellous tapestry through this life, all of us, all together. Ronald Blythe, in his book about the villagers of Akenfield, wrote that their...

> *...own life and the life of the corn and fruit and creatures clocks along with the same fatalistic movement. Spring-birth, winter-death and in between the harvest. This year, next year and forever – for that is the promise. Such inevitability cuts down on ambition and puts a brake on restlessness.*[55]

For the farmer, the year just keeps going; there is no end in sight. We can feel like this sometimes; it is easy to be overwhelmed at all there is to do in life, at all that lies before us, but as Jesus said, do not worry about tomorrow. We're not built to worry about what we cannot see. Be here now. This is it. It can feel like everything goes in circles. What goes around comes around, we say, but if we embrace the change and if we fall into the natural pattern of life then it will be easier. I'm thinking here of the unforced rhythms of grace that Jesus talked about.[56]

> *To the singing of the harvest-song goes the life of a year, or of all the years – the summer that is gone, the winter that is*

---

[54] Psalm 126:5 (NASB).
[55] Blythe, Ronald; *Akenfield;* Penguin, 2005 [1969] (p.15).
[56] See Matthew 11:28-30 (MSG).

*coming, the ones who have sown but are not here to reap; the
ones who will sow when the reapers that are have been
forgotten; the Good Being who makes the sun shine and the
corn ripen. There may be the breath of a sigh in that song, but
there is also in it a whole storm of rapture.*[57]

I see these natural rhythms reflected in my creativity. We have seasons
where one thing seems right and seasons for another. We start a project
and get sidetracked, and that's OK. Getting sidetracked is good for
creativity; it is often when we are not paying attention that we stumble
on to something new and unexpected. Have you noticed how your habits
change in the summer and winter? For me, winter is the time for
hibernation: cosying up by the fire and getting through the pile of books
that I accumulate through the year. I look forward to spring because
everything wakes up. The garden becomes beautiful, the birds start to
sing, the sun warms our skin, and I always feel like writing. The joy of
spring makes creativity well up in me. There is hope in the air. Here is a
little piece that I wrote about this:

It is the spring light that makes me want to write,
I swear each year it is the same.
This time, this light, the long evenings.
My hands becoming soft again,
my skin fixing itself again.
The light at the window gives me hope.
The older I grow, the more I see this life in circles.
I swear it's the same each year.

I find it fascinating finding out how other writers work to their own
rhythms. Roald Dahl was famous for his strict daily routine.

*He got up at the same time, he took the children to school, he
made his thermos of coffee, he answered his letters, he went
up to the hut, he worked to a certain time, he listened to the
World at One, he had his Bloody Mary.*[58]

---

[57] McLeod, Kenneth; *Celtic Daily Prayer;* Harper Collins, 2000 (p.296).
[58] Sturrock, Donald; *Storyteller: The Authorized Biography of Roald Dahl;*
Harper Collins, 2011 (p.462).

On January 8th each year, Isabelle Allende starts her next novel. She has seasons of research and then a season of writing.[59]

> *January 8 has been a lucky day for me. I have started all my books on that day, and all of them have been well received by the readers. I write eight to ten hours a day until I have a first draft, then I can relax a little. I am very disciplined. I write in silence and solitude.*[60]

What are the natural seasons within your creative year? Have you noticed times when you feel like researching, writing, finding inspiration and times when you feel like creating, whether it be writing, painting, singing, taking photographs, dancing? We are all unique and as such will all have different natural rhythms. Pay attention to yourself and find out what suits you best. For us to work at our best as creatives, we have to be aware of the rhythms that we work best to; what time of day is your most undisturbed and most creative? Could you do more to protect that time?

[59] Interview with Isabelle Allende in *Mslexia,* Issue 39, Oct/Nov/Dec 2008.
[60] Interview with Isabel Allende, May 2010; *www.goodreads.com.*

12

Look Up!

Burst

The things that I see and touch consume me;
the work that I must do,
the dinner that I must cook,
and the house that must be tidied
fill up the space in my mind.

And when I close my eyes,
all I can see is the bustle of things,
like a humming city, people and things to see and arrange.
So that it is even hard work to sit there and do nothing,
to think of stillness,
because things come so quickly to smudge away the quiet.

But there are times too,
when you cut through into my day,
when I am stepping off a kerb on to the road and I think of you.

When a customer smiles at me,
and it makes me feel unique,
and not just part of a machine.

When I look up and see a billboard that says 'Believe in More'
and it quietly stuns me on my walk into town.

When I see a leaf, lying on the pavement,
a glorious yellow on dull grey.

And what of all the ordinary things that we do?
The putting on of clothes,
the eating,
the washing of our faces,
the laughing,
the sulking?
Are you in that too?
In my mood swings, my tiredness,
my cold mornings and dark evenings?

And if you were not in the dawn,
the birdsong,
the sunrise,
the work,
the food,
the friends,
the pain,
the rest?

What would we do then?

THERE IS THE FINGERPRINT OF GOD EVERYWHERE WE LOOK, but sometimes life feels so mundane that we forget to look for the sublime, the wonderful. It can feel that we're always working to deadlines, always on the way somewhere, always with our heads down. With very young children, it felt like each day I was facing an assault course and sometimes I forgot to lift my eyes up. I found myself thinking, *God, I so need you but I don't have time to find you!*

Before I had children, I had not appreciated how all-consuming it would be, how utterly it would take over my life. It became a struggle to find time to come to God because I would fall into bed each night exhausted after a day of childcare, school drop-offs, after-school clubs, work and everything else in between. With children around, there is the moment the light goes out at bedtime and your head crashes exhausted into the pillow. Then you can pray. The morning doesn't work, because it is then that you are tugged from your bed by your hair at 6.30am. There are other times too, there is the pocket of space when you are driving, when they are not talking, there is the moment when they are watching TV.

When the children were all asleep, in the evening, my mind would be frantic with all that I could or should be doing. It became a struggle to worship because even at church, I wasn't off duty. In this season, I found that a lot of my prayers were for strength to keep going. A lot of my prayers were one-liners: 'God, give me strength.' 'Help me to stay patient.' 'Keep him safe.' 'I'm sorry.' I don't know of anything in my life that has tested me as thoroughly as being a mum that has taught me so much. One of the things I struggle with the most is keeping my thoughts coherent, but I treasure hearing the voice of God in my life and so I journal, because otherwise I would forget the important things that God has said to me. So whatever time constraints we have on our lives – caring for elderly family members, a demanding job, or a hectic family life – how can we learn to tune in to the voice of God? How can we tune our hearts to him? Many times, I have known the peace of God in a children's Bible story, the simplicity of the words ringing very true in my life. An example of this is the story of Exodus rewritten for the *Jesus Storybook Bible:*

> *But there's nothing we can do!*
>
> *God knows you can't do anything! God will do it for you. Trust him and watch!*
>
> *But there's no way out!*
>
> *God will make a way!* [61]

This was so encouraging to me in the midst of our difficult house move. But there are other things too, the blessings of creation, a nature documentary on television, an encouraging word from a friend, a song lyric that pops into your head that speaks directly into your situation. God walks this life with us, so he is there in the warmth of the sunshine, the birdsong; he is there in the exhaustion and the joy. I wonder why we are so keen to put the barriers up between spiritual life and natural life. It is his glorious creation, his world. Let's be alert, let's be expectant, let's always be listening for the gracious voice of God. He longs to speak with

---

[61] Lloyd-Jones, Sally; *The Jesus Storybook Bible;* Zondervan, 2007 (p.95).

us his precious children. Let's keep our eyes and ears wide open as we walk through today.

So my challenge to you today is to look up. Stop what you are doing for just a minute. What can you hear, what can you smell, how do you feel? Where can you see God? He is here with us every day. Why not write down five ways that help you to feel more connected to God? This could be watching the sunrise, going for a walk in the woods, swimming in an open-air swimming pool, or lighting a candle and sitting in silence. How can you make more time for these things? Let's make space in our lives for the holy; let's be expectant that God wants to speak into our lives at every stage. Let's live our lives in touch with and in awe of our creator.

13

Noise

SOMETIMES IT CAN FEEL LIKE LIFE IS AN ONSLAUGHT OF noise and information. I think we need to step back, to still the noise and quieten ourselves on occasions. Some mornings I sit down to work and the mere sight of my to-do list throws me into a quandary. There are so many things that I could do, how do I know what I *should* do? How do I split my time in the right way? How do I know what I should be focusing on? My mind is jittery and I can't get anything done until I slow down. I might put on a worship song and just journal all the thoughts that are causing my internal tornado. I feel peace when I come back to the source, to the Father, to the fountain that gives life.

As a creative today, it can feel that we have to juggle multiple personalities. As a writer, I need time to write, I also need projects with deadlines to keep me motivated, I also need to think about what might bring some money in, so I write articles and run workshops. I need to spend time hiding away, focusing on my 'seedling', but then there comes the time to emerge and to engage and draw in new customers in order to sell the art that I have spent so long creating. It can feel confusing!

Something I know that I can struggle with and that can really throw me off track is seeing the success of others all around me. Social media is an amazing tool but it needs to be managed in the right way. We can quickly become jealous of other's success and waste time scrolling through their feeds to find out how they have done it.

A verse from Isaiah illustrates the person who worships idols he has made for himself and the utter folly of this: *'such a person feeds on ashes'* [62]. This is like us when we turn to social media or the news before we turn to the truth of God's word. What we read, we are marinating in, we are feeding ourselves on. If that's how we start the day, then it's no

---

[62] Isaiah 44:20.

wonder that fear, insecurity and hopelessness will set in. Start the day instead by soaking in God's peace and truth, reminding yourself that he has a purpose for you, that he loves you deeply. Take a deep drink from the fountain that never runs dry and then turn to your work.

There are countless verses speaking of God as our fountain, our source of life. Psalm 36:8 calls us to *'feast on the abundance of [his] house,'* to *'drink from [his] river of delights. For with [him] is the fountain of life.'* We are reminded in Psalm 1 that the person who thinks about God's ways *'is like a tree planted by streams of water, which yields its fruit in season and whose leaf does not wither – whatever they do prospers'* [63]. We are talking about sustainability here! God is our life source; we cannot live if we are cut off from him!

---

[63] NIV.

14

Walking

WE ARE ALL ON A JOURNEY, AND EVERYONE HAS TO START out somewhere. I am convinced that our best tool as creatives is our uniqueness. So create whatever you have inside you to create, as you're the only one who has it. Even if it takes a little longer and even if you're tempted to jack it in. The honing process cannot be rushed so allow it time.

And when you have heard what your call is; when you have paid attention to the tears and the goosebumps, when you are on the right track, what then?

No one has said it will be easy; the creative road is one that is hard and you may see plenty of people walking seemingly easy paths alongside you. But if there's something in you that is struggling to be born, then you have to give it time to grow, time to be born.

Here is some advice that I have found really useful in my own creative path, and in my walk with God.

- Find your creative manifesto, the thing that reminds you why you get up in the morning. Have you found yours? If yes, great. If not, go looking for it, and when you find it, that thing that so rings true for you, then pin it up by the place where you work. It can be hard graft being a creative – we need cheering on sometimes.

- Keep feeding yourself. Often I read a piece of writing by, say, Ben Okri and am consumed with jealousy, thinking, 'I wish I'd written that.' But even better, and even more satisfying is when I read something and think, actually, I *could* have written that. It makes me realise I am on the right track and that I am getting to the heart of something.

- Keep coming back to God. Just ask him from time to time, 'Is there anything you want me to put down, or anything you want me to pick up?' Spending time with him will clarify our calling; it will sift out the silt. Many times, I have come to him and heard, 'Just keep doing what you're doing.' Sometimes things just need time.

- Don't worry about changing things. Steve Jobs, in his famous 2005 Stanford Commencement address, said:

For the past 33 years, I have looked in the mirror every morning and asked myself: 'If today were the last day of my life, would I want to do what I am about to do today?' And whenever the answer has been 'no' for too many days in a row, I know I need to change something.'

It is no failure to change things. Jobs continues:

Your work is going to fill a large part of your life, and the only way to be truly satisfied is to do what you believe is great work. And the only way to do great work is to love what you do. If you haven't found it yet, keep looking. Don't settle. As with all matters of the heart, you'll know when you find it. [...] So keep looking until you find it. Don't settle.[64]

- Don't worry about the big things but stay true to your heart. When I finished my undergraduate degree, I thought I wanted to work in publishing. But then I applied for a few jobs and didn't get anywhere and then I thought, *well, maybe I don't want to travel up to London every day. What I want to do is to study, and to learn to write.* So then I applied to the Creative Writing MA. And even when I was there, I didn't work on the student magazine because I wanted to wander around art galleries instead.

You can sometimes look at your life and think, *what am I doing here and how did I get here?* But then you realise that you have listened, and all along the line, at times you have thought, *this is ill-fitting,* and at times, *this fits just right,* and that is how we make our way along this road. For as Agnes de Mille says:

---

[64] Jobs, Steve; Stanford Commencement address, June 2005; reprinted in *The Observer,* Sunday 9 October 2011.

...no trumpets sound when the important decisions of our life are made. Destiny is made known silently. [65]

It's all just part of the journey. There are a thousand little decisions that we make all the way through life. It is deciding that this is really more important than that, that I am not willing to sacrifice this for that. And they are the little corrections that lead us to where we are now. That is not to say that we have arrived. Far from it, but it feels good to know where we have come from. It is in the slow shuffle and the long walk that we find our way. Oliver Burkeman in his column for the *Guardian* talked about the process of flying a plane and...

...for 90% of its journey, an aeroplane will be off course, yet it reaches its destination nonetheless. [66]

This is how we find our way; by walking day by day, step by step. Nelson Mandela ends his autobiography with these famous words:

...the secret to climbing a great hill is that there are many more to climb. I can rest only for a moment; with freedom comes great responsibilities and I dare not linger for my long walk has not ended. [67]

If there is a passion, a longing in you deep down to create, then hold on to that for dear life, because it is who you are, it is your wellspring of life:

Pay attention to the welfare of your innermost being, for from there flows the wellspring of life. [68]

Let's remember the verse we began with in Chapter 1, about the longing in God's children for pilgrimage, a longing to get back to the Father, to get back to our heavenly country, for those of us who have set our hearts on walking:

[65] Quoted in Cameron, Julia; *The Artist's Way;* Jeremy P. Tarcher / Putnam, 2002 [1992] (p.144).
[66] Oliver Burkeman; 'This column will change your life: the what-the-hell effect'; *The Guardian,* Saturday 24th May 2014.
[67] Mandela, Nelson; *Long Walk to Freedom;* Abacus, 1995.
[68] Proverbs 4:23 (TPT).

Blessed are those whose strength is in you, whose hearts are set on pilgrimage.[69]

---

[69] Psalm 84:5 (NIV).

15

Pick up Your Violin!

AS I HAVE ALREADY MENTIONED, I FIND THAT GOD SPEAKS to me through my children's story times quite often. It is then that I am half-asleep, I am not distracted, my defences are down, and for me that is sometimes the best time to hear God. The latest one is *Patrick* by Quentin Blake, a tale of wonder and music.

The message here is so strong that it leapt out at me as I read each line. To summarise: Patrick is a young man who sets out one day with his one silver piece to buy a violin. As he starts to play, wondrous things begin to happen all around him: fish start singing, cows start dancing, and ribbons sprout from a little girl's shoes. I think we can learn a lot from Patrick.

- He is single-minded. He wakes up and goes to buy a violin. He is not distracted by the other stalls at the market – he knows what he set out for.

- He gives up all he has for this violin (his only silver piece) and he receives it with joy.

- He can't wait to start using his gift:

    He was so pleased that he ran as fast as he could out into the fields. [...] Then he sat down by a pond and began to play a tune.[70]

    He uses it straight away; he doesn't hide his gift.

- As he starts to play his song, which is the thing that he is meant to be doing, the universe joins in. Fish start to sing, pigeons grow bright new feathers, cows start to dance, and trees grow ice creams

---

[70] Blake, Quentin; *Patrick;* from *The Quentin Blake Treasury;* Jonathan Cape, 2012 (pps.74-76).

and slices of hot-buttered toast. Everything is made more beautiful in the presence of the music. This reminds me of the principle of synchronicity in *The Artist's Way*, a fantastic book about creativity. Things start to happen when we're walking in the way that we should go. Julia Cameron says:

Once you accept that it is natural to create, you can begin to accept a second idea – that the creator will hand you whatever you need for the project. […] Expect the universe to support your dream.[71]

I'm not talking just about creativity here. It includes that, but it is more than that, it is who we are, whatever our gifts, whether hospitality, teaching, speaking different languages, woodwork. Whatever it is that makes us who we are.

- When faced with a situation that he doesn't know the answer to – the arrival of the ill and miserable tinker and his wife – Patrick uses his gift anyway. He says, *'Let me play my violin and see what happens.'*[72] In the presence of the music, the tinker gets fatter, loses his cough and his cold, and becomes happy again.

- Patrick has no control over the outcome and he isn't worried about that; he just does the part that he is responsible for: he uses his gift and plays.

- People are drawn to him as he releases joy – the two children, Kath and Mick; the tinker and his wife; all the animals and birds. They are all enjoying the journey and want to stay in the presence of the music and walk alongside Patrick. People keep company with those that are covered in glory. They want to see what is going to happen next.

To me, it is like a modern-day parable with lessons blazing out from it. I'm talking about going after the passions of our life, using our giftings boldly, living the life that we were created to live.

So what can we take from this?

---

[71] Cameron, Julia; *The Artist's Way*; Jeremy P. Tarcher / Putnam, 2002 [1992] (p.119).
[72] Blake, Quentin; *Patrick;* from *The Quentin Blake Treasury;* Jonathan Cape, 2012 (p.94).

- Be single minded – when you have found what it is that that you are meant to be doing, go after it single-heartedly. To some of us, God has given a gift of encouragement. Let's not just use it in the church but everywhere we go. To some, God has given a gift of music, or of cooking beautiful food. Whatever God has blessed you with, can I encourage you to give it away and to use it wherever you can? When we walk in our true identity, and we bless those around us, we are spreading the kingdom, and we are spreading God's love. In *Patrick,* the blessing that Patrick spreads is visible; in our day to day life, we may not always see it but it is happening nonetheless. 2 Corinthians 2:14 says:

But thanks be to God, who always leads us in triumph in Christ, and manifests through us the sweet aroma of the knowledge of Him in every place.[73]

This is what we take with us as we live our lives, the sweet aroma of the knowledge of him.

- Give up everything you have for the life that God has called you to live; it is worth it.

- When you receive your gift, use it all the time, in every situation that you can. Patrick starts to play the violin as soon as he receives it. We are so often scared to share what we have, believing that we aren't accomplished enough, but God loves our offerings and they can touch hearts.

- Patrick doesn't panic when he doesn't know what to do in a situation, and so don't worry about things that are beyond your control, just concentrate on what God has given you to do and see what happens. Life is a symphony and we can do just what we can do, and it all works together. Trust God that in this topsy-turvy life, he can use your offerings.

- If you are walking in the light of your true identity, people will see freedom and authenticity; they will be drawn to you. Your light will liberate others.

---

[73] NASB.

So close your eyes now. I want you to imagine that you are going to the market. Have a look around at all the stalls. Ask God if there is something for you to pick up, something that is just for you. You may have picked it up a long time ago, but maybe it is languishing in a dusty cupboard. You may be using it daily, just like Patrick. I went to the market a good few years ago and I saw a pen there waiting for me and I picked it up.

And once you have picked it up, put it to good use, and steward it well. Enjoy the unfolding of freedom all around you as you join in with heaven's symphony. Be bold and take steps to use your gift even though it takes courage. Last year, after my poems about motherhood were rejected for being 'good, but not quite good enough', I then decided to self-release a collection of hand-lettered versions of the poems. It didn't sit right with me that they were failures, doomed to gather dust on my laptop until the end of time. In my gut, I knew that they were valid and true. I sell them through my etsy shop and at craft fairs, and I have lost count of the number of times that someone has messaged me to say how much they loved a certain poem, or that a poem had really resonated with them. And for me, connecting with people is the reason why I write. So is it a failure to me that they were rejected and that I self-published the poems? Not in the least!

I am investing time into my gift, in honing and shaping it through a mentorship scheme. I am giving it away as I teach creative writing workshops. Let's not let these things lie dormant in us. Like in the parable of the talents, let's invest in our gifts and honour what God has given us. So I want to encourage you, is there anything else you can do to live in your giftings from day to day? I love the verse Galatians 6:4-5 that says:

> *Live creatively, friends. [...] Make a careful exploration of who you are and the work you have been given and sink yourself into that. Don't be impressed with yourself. Don't compare yourself with others. Each of you must take the responsibility for doing the creative best you can with your own life.*[74]

We can't compare ourselves because God has made us all different. So don't worry if your calling doesn't look like someone else's calling. Just listen to the voice of God and keep walking on your own path. I

---

[74] MSG.

think that church is a bit like a kitchen garden, a place that is sheltered from the wind, where there is good soil to grow. This is our safe space. So let's flourish here, and part of this is that we encourage each other. If there's something that you notice that someone has a real gift for, tell them! Kind words go a long way.

This quote from Marianne Williamson shows how we are all meant to be Patricks, walking joyfully down the road, using our gifts, watching the glory of God unfold around us.

> *Our deepest fear is not that we are inadequate. Our deepest fear is that we are powerful beyond measure. It is our light, not our darkness that most frightens us. We ask ourselves, who am I to be brilliant, gorgeous, talented, and fabulous? Actually, who are you not to be? You are a child of God. Your playing small does not serve the world. There is nothing enlightened about shrinking so that other people will not feel insecure around you. We are all meant to shine, as children do. We were born to make manifest the glory of God that is within us. It is not just in some of us; it is in everyone and as we let our own light shine, we unconsciously give others permission to do the same. As we are liberated from our own fear, our presence automatically liberates others.* [75]

So Lord, show each of us what you have given us to do. Help us to steward our gifts, help us to encourage one another to step out into new areas. May we grow well in this safe place that you have put us in. May we walk in freedom, setting those around us free.

---

[75] Williamson, Marianne; *A Return to Love: Reflections on the Principles of 'A Course in Miracles';* 1992 (Ch. 7, Section 3, p.190).

16

Longing

THERE'S A MOMENT IN LABOUR WHEN YOU'RE IN SO MUCH pain that it comes to clarity. It suddenly dawns on you that that the harder you push, the quicker the contractions will stop, and the sooner you will meet your baby. The pain turns to desperation which turns to action. Just the other night I was crying out to God about my daughter, telling God that I don't understand why she has to live with her condition. It seems to me that sometimes we need the pain to stay grounded, to make us care. We have our burdens in this life, the weights that our hearts carry. These are the things that we can offer up to God in prayer, but sometimes the weight of them keeps returning to us. We named our daughter Ivy June and then we realised that her name meant 'faithful warrior', and then we found out that she had something to fight against.

But sometimes these burdens that we hold so close and we so long for are those prayers that we have said a thousand times to God. We feel like our longing has got us nowhere, but he counts our prayers and he remembers them. Revelation 5:8 says that in heaven the elders fall before the lamb, *'each one holding a harp and golden bowls full of incense, which are the prayers of the saints'* [76]. A well-known story of longing in the Bible is that of Zechariah and Elizabeth who desperately wanted a child. In his old age, Zechariah is visited by an angel who says, *'Do not be afraid, Zechariah; your prayer has been heard.'* [77]

Vincent's Word Studies puts it like this:

Is heard (ε ἰσηκ οὐσθη)...

---

[76] NASB.
[77] Luke 1:13 (NIV).

If we render the aorist literally, was heard, we avoid the question as to what prayer is referred to. The reference is to the prayer for offspring, which, owing to His extreme years, Zacharias had probably ceased to offer, and which he certainly would not be proffering in that public and solemn service. Hence the aorist is appropriate, referring back to the past acts of prayer. 'That prayer, which thou no longer offerest, was heard.' [78]

The prayer which we have stopped praying. Maybe because we are too tired or we have lost faith, but God is not like us. He hears and he remembers, and he still holds our prayers before him.

This longing can be carried over into our artistic lives too. Lawrence Calcagno, a painter said:

As an artist, it is central to be unsatisfied! This isn't greed, though it might be appetite. [79]

If we aren't there yet with our creativity, then there is a longing that runs deeper than earning a living or making ends meet; it is about who we are and why we are alive. In Hebrews there is a wonderful passage about all of this, about a people who were on the journey but not there yet, about a people who were longing for their own country:

All these great people died in faith. They did not get [receive] the things that God promised his people, but they saw them coming far in the future [from afar] and were glad [welcomed/greeted them]. They said they were like strangers [foreigners] and visitors [sojourners; refugees; resident aliens] on earth. When people say such things, they show they are looking for a country that will be their own [homeland]. If they had been thinking about the country they had left, they could have gone back. But they were waiting [desiring; longing] for a better country – a heavenly one. So God is not ashamed to be called their God, because he has prepared a city for them. [80]

---

[78] Vincent's Word Studies; *http://biblehub.com/commentaries/vws/luke/1.htm.*

[79] Quoted in Cameron, Julia; *The Artist's Way;* Jeremy P. Tarcher / Putnam, 2002 [1992] (p.114).

[80] Hebrews 11:13-16 (The Expanded Bible).

The word translated here as *'waiting'* is the Greek word *oregó* which means 'to stretch out, to reach after, to yearn for'.[81] It is this active waiting, this stretching out towards, that is true longing.

Longing

You speak to me of longing,
and it seems a thing I don't yet know.
I longed for a child, the first,
I longed for a garden.
But I knew you before I longed for you
and my daughter
and my second son were gifts of grace to me.
I don't long for my writing,
because I feel that there is time,
I don't feel rushed and that is a grace.
But you are unfulfilled,
because you are not yet in the land, and
you have been walking for a long time.
You long for it each day.
And this longing is a precious thing,
it is a holy fire,
it burns away
all that is peripheral,
unneeded.

We carry these burdens through our days but we are called to keep giving them back to Jesus. He says:

> *Come to me, all you who are weary and burdened, and I will give you rest. Take my yoke upon you and learn from me, for I am gentle and humble in heart, and you will find rest for your souls. For my yoke is easy and my burden is light.*[82]

It is my experience that God is moved by us being radically real with him, taking down all the walls, laying all of our heart cries at his feet. He

---

[81] *http://biblehub.com/greek/3713.htm.*
[82] Matthew 11:28-30 (NIV).

wants our loves, our passions, the truth of who we are. There are two times in my life when I have seen this. One was before we had children and were wasting money on rent when it was really on our hearts to get a mortgage. We were going through the Shared Ownership scheme, sharing a purchase with the council, and we had been on the list for a year and had applied for several properties. It suddenly came to a point of crisis for me and I literally cried out to God, saying, *what are we doing here, where are we going?* The very next morning, we received a phone call saying that the house we wanted was ours. The other time was when we wanted to start a family but I couldn't get pregnant. Again, I just gave God my heart, I made it all real with him, I didn't pretend. And the next month I fell pregnant. It was such a grace to me. Sadly, I know it's not always this easy, and many of us will live for many years with unfulfilled longings and unanswered prayers. But these two times, it surprised me to the core. I felt like I just had a major tantrum with God and something shifted. Maybe there is power in our longing to change things.

So may we long with all of our being for our life source, may we be real with him and seek him with all that we are.

> *O God, You are my God; I shall seek You earnestly;*
> *My soul thirsts for You, my flesh yearns for You,*
> *In a dry and weary land where there is no water.*[83]

I love the physicality of this psalm. It is a literal longing, as for water, as for the very source of life.

So we will long, and in a sense our lives will always be made up of longing for we aren't there yet, we aren't in our heavenly country, but may these desires in our hearts, the ones that have been sown in us by our Father, come to fruition; may all the years of hard graft and sowing result in a rich bounty of fruit for *'hope deferred makes the heart sick, but desire fulfilled is a tree of life'*[84]. So may we pray for blessing on our creativity, may we see longing turn to fruit and not just meagre fruit but bounty, for such is the way of things with God.

> *You care for the land and water it;*
> *you enrich it abundantly.*
> *The streams of God are filled with water*
> *to provide the people with grain,*

---

[83] Psalm 63:1 (NASB).
[84] Proverbs 13:12 (NASB).

for so you have ordained it.
You drench its furrows and level its ridges;
you soften it with showers and bless its crops.
You crown the year with your bounty,
and your carts overflow with abundance.
The grasslands of the wilderness overflow;
the hills are clothed with gladness.
The meadows are covered with flocks
and the valleys are mantled with grain;
they shout for joy and sing.[85]

The rough and long road makes us long so much for the fruit of what we have been working for. If there is something that is being birthed in us, we long for it to come to life. If we are in labour, we long to meet our child; if our child is ill, we long for their healing. And this longing is like magnetism, it draws us back to the feet of the Father.

---

[85] Psalm 65:9-13 (NIV).

17

Letting Go

AFTER THE STRUGGLE, THERE IS A RELIEF MIXED WITH FEAR when we break through. Imagine pushing with all your might against a wall and then one day it gives way. Suddenly you are terrified. You used all your strength against that wall, that was just the way it was, then all of a sudden there is space. There was the next step.

When I have finished a work, there are several steps that I go through. A sigh of relief ('I've done it! I can't believe I got to the end!'), a wave of terror ('Maybe it's not quite finished, maybe it's not good enough…'), a sense of exhaustion ('It felt like a marathon and now I need to recover'), a sense of dread ('What next?'). These are the stages that we work through. We might leave our work to rest for a while, we might seek feedback from others, we might launch it and see what the world thinks.

I have spent a good many years (about ten!) working on a novel, off and on. Last year, after writing, redrafting, getting a mentor, reworking, redrafting, polishing, I began to send out the first three chapters to agents. It felt a curious thing. I had finished at last. I could breathe a sigh of relief. I was proud of what I had achieved. But I also found myself stepping back from it. It was its own thing, launched into the inboxes of strangers.

It felt a bit like labour; there was the exhaustion and the elation but then there was this thing that you had created. You finally got to meet your child for the first time and it was kind of surprising. There was a new being, entirely apart from you. When my first son was born, and as he grew, I naively thought we would be able to pin each part of him down; 'You get that from your father, that from me,' 'We thought you'd be like this.' But he was utterly different, utterly surprising. I guess that's how I feel about the novel; it is a thing that I gave birth to, but it is a thing set apart from me.

On some of the agent's submission pages, I had to explain why I wrote the novel, how it filled a gap in the market, and what I could compare it to, but I was a little stumped at these questions. I didn't write to fill a gap, or because I was knowledgeable about a certain thing; I wrote it because it came up out of me.

There is always a mixture of things that go into a novel – a culmination of interests, of curiosity from my childhood, strange tales from my father, an attempt to make sense of those things that don't make sense, especially in the mind of a child – but I think we are drawn to certain things subconsciously and only the unfolding of time will tell us why. Or maybe we will never know why. I remember a piece of writing that I was really pleased with at secondary school. It was a description of my grandmother's garden, the tumbledown sheds, the willow that you could hide yourself in, and it stayed with me, the mystery of that place. It seemed like something I could write about. There are layers and layers of memories in that garden; tasting juicy apples straight from the tree, learning to roll the old rusty barrel under my feet, my uncle pulling an armchair out on to the lawn in the blazing sun. And these layers have settled down over time to create a rich source of material, of feeling and memory, of detail which comes back when I start to dig.

And there are other influences too; who I am now, and also the mystery of creativity, the life force of the work itself which tugs and pulls your story in ways that you were not expecting. And when this starts to happen, when my own writing surprises me, if feels as if I am finally getting somewhere.

For letting go happens all the time in creativity, not just at the end when we finally show it to others, but all the way through, if we let it...

18

If Only…

IT'S EASY FOR US TO SAY, IF ONLY I DIDN'T HAVE CHILDREN, if only I weren't so tired, if only I had more money, then I'd be able to create. In a fantastic book called *Happier,* the author illustrates a study that proves that our level of happiness is not determined by what we have or do not have, but something else:

> *Within as short a period as a month, lottery winners return to their base levels of well-being – if they were unhappy before winning, they will remain so.*[86]

'If only' is a myth to keep you from your life's work. 'Little and often' is my mantra for these days. I don't say *every day* because for me that takes the grace out of it. I want to want to write; I don't want it to turn into cello practice. (I still remember the churn of my stomach when I had to go and practise. It killed it for me, I think.) So I don't want my writing to die. But equally, I don't want to keep putting it off, imagining a better situation. In fact, I can't imagine a better situation. This is it.

So if our life is what we have in our hands, what can we do, except to pray that we hear the Father's guidance, that we steward well this gift that he has bestowed on us, that we stay thankful, that we stay hungry?

One of the quotes on my writing room wall is attributed to Thoreau. In fact, it must mean a lot to me because it is up there twice:

> *Go confidently in the direction of your dreams! Live the life you've imagined. As you simplify your life, the laws of the universe will be simpler.*[87]

---

[86] Ben-Shahar, Tal; 'Happier'; *The Observer,* 2008 (p.68).
[87] Quoted in Cameron, Julia; *The Artist's Way;* Jeremy P. Tarcher / Putnam, 2002 [1992] (p.38).

Once, stuck at a point of 'Where do I go next? How do I progress with this?', I felt God say to live as I wanted to be living. *Live as a poet.* If I were living as a poet, what would I do next? If I knew that that was my identity, where would I dare to tread? If there were no fear, in other words, if that was who I am. There is much more that could be said about this: our identity in Christ. There is one who comes to steal and to destroy, so if you are thinking, *who am I to be an artist,* then perhaps you are listening to the wrong voice. I'm thinking back to that Marianne Williamson quote, *'Who are you not to be?'* As children of God, we were created to shine.

Raymond Carver is another one of my heroes cheering me on from my great cloud of witnesses. In his essay 'Fires', he says that the exhaustion and relentlessness of bringing up small children and trying to make ends meet had the greatest influence on his writing career. The stories became what they were because of his life:

> *My children are it. Theirs is the main influence. They were the prime movers and shapers of my life and my writing.*[88]

These children make us, they make life worth living, they mould and shape us as artists and creators, and their imprint will forever be on our creations. So whatever trying circumstance you face, lack of money or time, stress, illness, there is always a little space to be made. There is room even in all of this to take a step towards your creativity, to breathe a little bit of heaven.

Today I challenge you to read that Thoreau quote again. Maybe even pin it up somewhere and read it each day. What liberty to be told to go in the direction of your dreams! What could you do today to take one step towards the direction of your dreams, if you were given permission? Allow me to give you permission today. Book into a sewing class, take a walk in the woods, buy a new journal and pen? Make that step today. And if you were to live as a poet (substitute here whatever you are aiming for: dancer, painter, musician), what would you do today? How would you live differently today?

Start small; it is empowering to pay it forwards, to give away your creativity, it is a gift. As a struggling creative, there can be a real frustration in the works that you have spent hours and hours in creating, when after all that they get rejected several times and just sit on your

---

[88] Carver, Raymond; 'Fires'; an essay from *Fires;* Vintage, 2009 (p.39).

laptop. It feels like we need to pass it on for it to flow and not to stagnate. But there is always something we can do. There is the Internet which gives us an immediate network. If you are a writer, consider starting a blog. There is self-publishing. Likewise, musicians and choreographers have a potentially enormous audience due to the power of the Internet. I worked with a charity in Guildford to run a spontaneous writing booth at a 'mind, body, spirit' fair, writing and giving away poems on demand. I have given a writing workshop in an elderly people's home. I run a Saturday writing workshop and after school clubs. There are always ways that you can live in your giftings and that you can give them away. Look around.

19

Sticks and Stones: The Power of Words

WE HAVE TO BE A LITTLE BIT CRAZY TO HAVE A DREAM. AND that is OK. It takes singlemindedness to hold on to something that might not reap any rewards for a long time. And all this time, well-meaning friends and family might keep enquiring, 'So when are you going to get a real job?', 'When are you going to get on to the property ladder?' And after you have justified yourself for the hundredth time, you may start to doubt your intentions, thinking, *hang on, why am I doing this, surely there's an easier way?* For my husband and me, who are both desperately pursuing a creative life, it's doubly painful and embarrassing to have to justify both of your decisions time and time again. In fact, you sometimes want everyone to leave you alone until you make it, whatever 'make it' means. I think we need thick skins as artists, and the trouble is that as creatives, we are often emotional people. For the sake of self-preservation, we need to ignore some people and we also need to hold firm to the reason why we are doing what we do.

I have been thinking lately about the things that people say to us, the bad and the good, and the way that we carry these words around like a rucksack for the rest of our lives, rifling through it to pull out the appropriate words at those crucial fight or flight moments. I remember fishing for compliments at the end of my Art GCSE from my teacher.

'Do you think I could do Art at A-Level?' I asked, looking for a good word to put in my rucksack.

She leant on my table and 'ummed' for a good while before saying, 'You could...' in a slightly less than enthusiastic tone.

Needless to say, I didn't take Art at A-level and haven't touched it since. (Not until I started hand-lettering and illustrating my poems.) But every now and then a little voice inside me speaks up and says it wants to take an art class and another voice shouts it down saying, 'You aren't validated! Who are you to think you can paint?' But who are we *not* to?

And why do we put such limits on our lives? And what if there is in fact no limit, no ceiling?

As a girl at my gymnastics class, I put myself forward to be in the junior routine. I was asked if I could do a backwards somersault and I said yes, launching myself down the runway to perform the lowest somersault my coach said she had ever seen, to giggles from the team. I didn't perform in the junior routine. I played cello too, and once, whilst at rehearsals for a school concert, I put myself forward to perform a solo piece. I don't think it crossed my mind to be afraid until several people came up to me and said, 'Are you sure?' And my response was, 'Oh, OK, maybe I won't.' They were memories that still make me cringe today and I think that quite a few times in my youth, I was wary of punching above my weight; in fact, since then I probably haven't punched anywhere near my weight. What is that old chestnut – sticks and stones may break my bones but words can never hurt me? It's not true, is it?

Words; the good and the bad come back to find us in the anxious times, and for some reason we hold on to some more than others. Something that my mother used to say about happiness, that she has repeated to me over the years, is that it is the little things in life that matter most – like buttered toast and poached eggs for tea on a Sunday, like going for a walk in the sunshine. We find happiness by feeling connection to this earth, and we stay rooted by really smelling, tasting and touching. Happiness is enjoying the journey – sometimes we need to stop looking at the bigger picture. This was remarkably helpful to me in times of doubt in my twenties – as I questioned why on earth I was trying to pursue a career in writing when all my friends had sensible jobs, and on wondering what my life was about. Remember, it is about the little decisions that we make every day, the things that we prioritise. This is how we get to where we want to go.

Words can break down walls, they can crush dreams, they can build people up. A friend enquired what I was up to after my MA and when I told him I was writing a novel, he laughed at me. It's just not seen as a serious option to be creative; in fact, it's often seen as ridiculous. I think when you are bringing something new and wonderful to life, and you are a sensitive soul, you sometimes have to keep secrets. Our newly flourishing art is like a child; it needs a safe place to blossom. I think we have a degree of responsibility in this in that we can surround ourselves with people that will support us, not laugh at us. If there is someone who you know is likely to be critical, then don't share your latest artistic creation with them in its infancy. Don't let it be trampled on before it has had time to take flight.

And equally, when you have found people who support your creativity, share and encourage them too. Your words have immense and far-reaching power. Don't underestimate the power of them. Proverbs says:

> Reckless words pierce like a sword, but the tongue of the wise brings healing.[89]

I had a revelation a few years ago when I was really feeling the weight of being 'foolish'. We were living in an expensive part of the South East of England and both struggling artists. I had spent a small fortune on my Master's in Creative Writing and we were squeezed in a small house with two young children. I felt like God said to me, 'You aren't foolish; you are wise because you have valued what I have sown into you.' And then I thought of the parable of the talents and I said then, 'Far be it from me to bury what you have given to me.'

Because, after all, what are we living for? Is it for the praise of man or to become the person our heavenly father has made us to be? I know my answer.

So how can we keep going?

- Find your manifesto. Ask God for a promise or a verse to cling to. Write it out, pin it up.

- Ask yourself what you are aiming for. Is it to write music to be performed? Is it to have a book published? Is it to create a dance? Write it out, pin it up.

- Surround yourself with those who will support your dreams.

- Keep walking.

---

[89] Proverbs 12:18 (NIV).

20

Joining the Dots

SO WHERE DOES ALL THIS LEAVE US? I DON'T HAVE ALL THE answers, for I am still walking too. But I know and I have seen that as we walk we grow.

We have to learn to follow our heart, as Frederick Buechner says; it will tell us more about ourselves than we know. Maybe we have to follow intuition for a while instead of reason. Marc Chernoff, life coach says:

> *Intuition is very real and something that is never wise to ignore, because it comes from deep within your subconscious and is derived from your previous life experiences. If everyone else is telling you "yes" but your gut is telling you otherwise, it's usually for a good reason. When faced with difficult decisions, seek out all the information you can find, become as knowledgeable as you possibly can, and then listen to your God-given instincts.[90]*

Steve Jobs, in his Stanford Commencement address, talks about the time he became disillusioned with college but he hung around and took a few optional classes. In retrospect, he says:

> *It was one of the best decisions I ever made. The minute I dropped out I could stop taking the required classes that didn't interest me, and begin dropping in on the ones that looked interesting [...] much of what I stumbled into by following my curiosity and intuition turned out to be priceless later on.*

The calligraphy class that he took ended up influencing the way that the typeface on Macs was designed.

---

[90] *www.marcandangel.com/2014/12/14/7-rituals-you-should-steal-from-extremely-creative-people.*

There is an essence of blind faith about all of this. Sometimes we think, *well, this doesn't make sense,* but we have to trust that it is all working together. Jobs says:

> *You can't connect the dots looking forward; you can only connect them looking backwards. So you have to trust that the dots will somehow connect in your future. You have to trust in something – your gut, destiny, life, karma, whatever.*[91]

As a Christian, I believe that *'God works all things together for the good of those who love him'*[92]. I pray Psalm 90:17 on a regular basis: *'Let the beauty of the Lord our God be upon us and establish the work of our hands, yes establish the work of our hands,'*[93] for he longs with the same longing as us to see our desires fulfilled, and he is a lavish father who gives good gifts to his children.

> *Every good and perfect gift is from above, coming down from the Father of the heavenly lights, who does not change like shifting shadows.*[94]

An interesting blog I came across recently posted an article entitled '12 Quiet Rituals of Enormously Successful Humans'[95]. One of the insights was that success is loud, but to get there takes a lot of work in the background, a lot of quiet work. This, Susan Cain argues in *Quiet,* is the introverts' main strength:

> *The trick is not to amass all the different kinds of available power but to use well the kind you've been granted. Introverts are offered keys to private gardens full of riches.*[96]

And also the fact that introverts are…

---

[91] Jobs, Steve; Stanford Commencement address, June 2005; reprinted in *The Observer,* Sunday 9 October 2011.
[92] Romans 8:28 (BSB).
[93] (NKJV).
[94] James 1:17 (NIV).
[95] *www.marcandangel.com.*
[96] Cain, Susan; *Quiet;* Penguin, 2012 (p.266).

> *...relatively unmotivated by rewards gives you incalculable power to go your own way. It's up to you to use that independence to good effect.*[97]

As artists with a mandate, we need sometimes to put our heads in the sand and just get on with our own dreams until they are ready to fly.

As Lewis Hyde says in *The Gift,* we need to pass our creativity on to stop it becoming blocked up, there needs to be an outlet for it to remain healthy. It just makes me wonder in our churches, how many stifled creatives are there? It's time to start dreaming of how we can use our gifts, like Quentin Blake's *Patrick,* how we can walk in our giftings and make this a part of our day-to-day lives. What will it take for us to realise that we are free to walk in our calling? For me, as a writer, how can I live this out in my community, in my life right now, today? How can I take my life into my hands and be proactive about using what God has given me? I have started to teach Creative Writing as well as writing, revising and submitting my own work, and it does feel healthy to be able to 'pay it forward', to pass on my passion for self-expression and to see it released in others. It's all about hushing that voice calling out, 'Who do you think you are!' And the only way to hush is it to start speaking with our own true voice. There is a degree of taking responsibility for our own lives here. Erica Jong famously said:

> *Take your life in your own hands and what do you have? A terrible thing: no one to blame.*[98]

I was recently reading 2 Corinthians and it struck me how chapters 3, 4 and 5 seem to illustrate this creative call. Firstly, there is the artist, freely creating, assured of his calling, creating heavenly works. He shares these and opens the flow of his creativity. People are touched and astounded by the work, the feel of it, the innocence, the other-worldliness:

> *Through us spreads everywhere the fragrance of the knowledge of him. For we are to God the aroma of Christ among those who are being saved and among those who are*

---

[97] *Ibid.* (p.173).
[98] Quoted in Cameron, Julia; *The Artist's Way;* Jeremy P. Tarcher / Putnam, 2002 [1992] (p.74).

perishing. To the one we are the smell of death; to the other, the fragrance of life.[99]

The fragrance of life! And the work and the artist reflect the glory of God:

Now the Lord is the Spirit, and where the Spirit of the Lord is, there is freedom. And we all, who with unveiled faces contemplate the Lord's glory, are being transformed into his image with ever-increasing glory, which comes from the Lord, who is the Spirit.[100]

The artist is a cracked pot, a lowly vessel, but takes pride in this because it is God who is glorified, not us.

We have this treasure in jars of clay to show that this all-surpassing power is not from God and not from us.[101]

And still the artist longs for his heavenly dwelling:

We groan, longing to be clothed with our heavenly dwelling because when we are clothed we will not be found naked. For while we are in this tent we groan and are burdened because we do not wish to be unclothed but to be clothed with our heavenly dwelling, so that what is mortal may be swallowed up in life.[102]

But while here on earth, he knows that this is his work, the message of reconciliation:

We are therefore Christ's ambassadors as though God were making his appeal through us.[103]

So our mandate, our creative call, is to taste of the mystery and glory of heaven and to show it to those around us in the work that we produce, to say, *come and drink, come and see that the Lord is good.* This is the longing that is within us. And that longing will remain and it will burn like a fire, until all that remains is precious silver and gold.

---

[99] 2 Corinthians 3:14-16 (NIV).
[100] 2 Corinthians 3:17,18 (NIV).
[101] 2 Corinthians 4:7 (NIV).
[102] 2 Corinthians 5:2-4 (NIV).
[103] 2 Corinthians 5:20 (NIV).

But each man must be careful how he builds. [...] Now if any man builds on the foundation with gold, silver, precious stones, wood, hay, straw, each man's work will become evident; for the day will show it because it is to be revealed with fire, and the fire itself will test the quality of each man's work.[104]

So let us build our lives with silver and gold, with all the beauty of the tapestry of heaven. For we see in part and we see threads of light, we see clouds parting, we see shades of glory. It is about the circles of what has gone before; it is about walking humbly with our God, about living each day under the banner of his new name for us; it is about longing, for we are strangers and exiles here on this earth, we are longing for the fullness, for our heavenly country. And part of the mystery is that we are trying to say what words cannot say, we're trying to paint the unpaintable, to say the unsayable, to make new and unheard-of sounds, to dance unseen dances, to make new what has not been before, to bring into this world something that it is longing for but doesn't yet know it.

---

[104] 1 Corinthians 3:10-13 (NIV).

21

Full Circle

LIFE GOES IN CIRCLES; WE CAN FEEL THAT WE ARE GETTING nowhere, that nothing is ever changing, when really things are evolving and we are advancing, little by little. Set goals for yourself, reflect and see where you are in a year's time. Make note of the things that you have stepped out in, and the things that have become less scary. Personally, I see advancements in years, not in months or weeks. Because of the restrictions of time that I have, things seem to take me longer, but I am at peace with that because that it just my stage of life. To-do lists are my friend, as is my journal. If I look back over a year, I can see how it really has shaped my workings; there are things that I have written on wish lists in there, that now I have actually done. It has shaped my thinking and given me achievable goals. There are many more on the list and there is also the great unknown. What happens next, what is the next step, what is the next project? What area do you want me to grow in next, God? But at the moment, I am happy to live this day and then the next, the knowing is not for me to know yet, and I am enjoying the pilgrimage, the journey from unknown to unknown, I am enjoying the slow blossoming of all that he has made me to be.

So allow yourself. Discover, take steps, start the journey. What's the worst that could happen?

Today is the first day.

Related Books from the Publisher

Hit the Ground Running
Hilary Jane Hughes
ISBN 978-1-907509-78-0

Hilary's poems describe life in its fullness – its beauty, its pain, its purpose. Through the highs and lows of life's journey the author openly expresses the deep emotions and questions faced by her, but also an eternal hope that keeps her moving forwards. Here are fifty-five pieces, varied in length and focus. Some are raw and restless, others sentimental, whimsical or quirky and yet others a pouring out of love from the heart and from God. The author's hope is they will inspire readers to be real about themselves, to press on in their faith, to own their gifts and use them for others and for the Lord.

www.onwardsandupwards.org/hit-the-ground-running

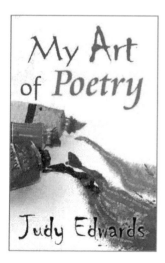

My Art of Poetry
Judy Edwards
ISBN 978-1-907509-03-2

Art and poetry have been at the heart of Judy Edwards. Through these media, this book expresses her love for God and his creation as experienced from her home in the southwest of England. Judy's poems, birthed during an ongoing battle against ME, are nonetheless uplifting and encouraging, founded on hope and timeless values of the Christian faith.

www.onwardsandupwards.org/my-art-of-poetry

23736048R00056

Printed in Great Britain
by Amazon